SOUND WISDOM BOOKS BY JIM ROHN

The Power of Ambition

The Art of Exceptional Living

AN OFFICIAL NIGHTINGALE CONANT PUBLICATION

UNSHAKABLE

BUILDING YOUR
INDESTRUCTIBLE FOUNDATION
FOR PERSONAL AND PROFESSIONAL SUCCESS

JIM ROHN

Published and distributed by:
SOUND WISDOM
P.O. Box 310
Shippensburg, PA 17257-0310
717-530-2122

info@soundwisdom.com

www.soundwisdom.com

ISBN 13 TP: 978-1-64095-359-8

ISBN 13 eBook: 978-1-64095-360-4

For Worldwide Distribution, Printed in the U.S.A.

5 6 7 8 / 26 25 24

CONTENTS

Introduction

YOUR INNER RESOURCES

I n this book, we explore the twelve qualities that I believe are the bedrock of unshakable character traits that lead to personal and professional success. We look at *courage* to do the right thing. *Integrity* is discussed and why doing the right thing is always in your best interest. *Honesty* is considered and you will see why it is always best to being honest with yourself. We examine *perseverance* and see how it can overcome virtually any challenge.

The quality of *wisdom* is discussed and you will see why knowing the facts of a situation isn't always the same as knowing the truth. Another quality is personal *responsibility* and why, like Harry Truman, you should adopt a "Buck stops here" mentality. You will see how *humor* is an enjoyable trait and why people of character know the importance of being able to laugh at themselves.

Flexibility is defined to see why it is more important today than ever before. You will discover why *patience* really is a virtue—one we need to take seriously. *Confidence* is inspiring yourself to take the first step in leading others. *Good health* is explored, confirming how a strong body and mind contribute to strong character. Also discussed is the true nature of *achievement* and you will see why it can't really be measured except in your own heart.

SUCCESS IS WITHIN YOUR REACH

Despite all of the huge changes that have taken place worldwide and in the United States—increased competition from other countries, the falling cost of labor in the world economy, and the revolution wrought by high technology—America is still the land of opportunity. Still the one place where everything you need for success is within reach. Today you still have a real chance to turn your dreams into reality—no matter who you are or where you start.

Some people may disagree with me about that. But I know it's true. That is why we should be doing everything we can to make the most of the opportunities that have been given to us. Of course, lots of men and women are doing just that. I've seen success happen for a great many people. And I would like to think that along the way I've helped some of them—and will help you as well.

Let's look for a moment at some of the important changes that have taken place in the world. For one thing, more people have access to the spectrum of technological advances. There are cars in garages and computers, satellite dishes, etc. And I say, "Good!" Because when you have worked hard for it and you have it, having nice stuff is fun.

But I also say, "Take care." Or maybe even, "Beware!"— because what really matters can get buried under everything else. The right stuff can get smothered under all the plastic and shiny gadgets.

Only your inner resources will sustain you. When the clock strikes midnight and the carriage turns into a pumpkin, even your inner strength and goals can start to get lost. What you have becomes a little less important than what you are.

I'm talking about character. I'm talking about leadership, too. The ability to inspire yourself that qualifies you, that gives you the right, that makes you worthy to lead others and enjoy healthy relationships.

Does it seem to you that a lot of people are succeeding these days without the benefit of a strongly developed character? It seems that way to me sometimes.

But I think some very positive signs are beginning to appear. I think we are starting to realize that we had better remember what got us this far if we expect to go any farther. And because you are reading my words right now, I know you understand the importance of character. You are the kind of person I had in mind when I decided to write a book that reveals the major ideas I've learned about character and leadership.

You are the one I want to talk to—and I am glad that you have decided to join me.

1

CHARACTER AND COURAGE

CHARACTER

I find it especially helpful when I discover something about the origins of words in ancient or foreign languages. For example, when I began planning to write about the topic of *character,* I looked up the word in the dictionary, and in this case the origin of the word just about says it all. I hope it has as big of an effect on you as it did on me.

But first, I quickly want to mention the origin of the word "charisma," which people often confuse with character. *Charisma* is derived from a Greek word meaning "an ability to elicit favor in other people." It is a magnetic quality of personality that people respond to as if it were magic. Charisma is almost like a magic wand that confers power over others.

But "character" has a very different origin. *Character* comes from a Greek word meaning chisel, or the mark left by a chisel. I think that is very important. A chisel is a sharp steel tool used for making a sculpture out of hard or difficult material like granite or marble. And the chisel is also used for stripping away waste materials, stuff that might get in the way of essentials—what really matters in life.

So in their origins, the words "character" and "charisma" are not related. You have to chisel your character out of the raw material of yourself, just like a sculptor creates a statue. The raw material is always there; and everything that happens to you, good or bad, is an opportunity for you to build or chisel out your personal character.

Let me point out another important distinction between character and charisma. You may have noticed it already. In both its definition and derivation, character doesn't refer to other people. It doesn't refer to having power over other people or getting other people to follow you, or gaining favor with other people.

Character is something that you have and that you are. You could be marooned on a desert island and your character would still be important. In fact, it would likely be *very* important in that situation. But charisma wouldn't do you any good at all. Charisma requires the presence of others, while character is all about you.

Character is the person you are after you have chiseled and chiseled, and have moved past all of the unnecessary qualities to what is important deep down. Because we are usually surrounded by other people, let me be a little more specific about how the differences between a charismatic person and a person with character can play out in the real world—particularly in leadership situations.

The following are four sets of circumstances that can easily occur.

First, a really charismatic person can make people believe their pie-in-the-sky scenario, or that the sky is going to fall tomorrow. One just as easily as the other. By creating these expectations, charismatic individuals can, indeed, energize and inspire others—or terrify and demotivate them until the overblown scenarios are proven false and the charisma runs its course. But a person of character doesn't need to be any-one's Pied Piper and isn't comfortable in that role. Instead, he or she looks within for the true source of inspiration and energy.

Second, a charismatic person can inspire devoted or even fanatical loyalty. But this can all too easily turn into an uncon-scious sense of dependency. That can make matters difficult when the leader is no longer available. Like a charismatic coach, effective during the glory years, but when he leaves the organization there is a sense of abandonment. The team may never achieve anything like its prior success. Powerful personalities often resist delegating authority. But it is an atti-tude of character for a leader to refrain from making himself or herself the indispensable heart and soul of an organization.

The *third* difference between character and charisma that is particularly important in a leadership situation is that char-ismatic people have to keep pulling rabbits out of the hat. The magic of their presence has to keep expressing itself or people might start wondering where it went. Worse yet, they might get bored.

For example, during World War II, US General Dwight Eisen-hower was picked to command the Allied Forces in Europe. Not because he was an exciting leader with a sense of high drama. But precisely because he wasn't. There were plenty of charismatic individuals around such as UK Prime Minister

Winston Churchill, British General Bernard Montgomery, French General Charles De Gaulle, and US General George Patton. What was needed was somebody with toughness, stamina, and the ability to manage people.

Just before the Normandy Invasion in 1944, Eisenhower met with a group of officers who would be going into battle. He stretched out a piece of string on a table and pulled it a few inches with his finger. "An army, is like this piece of string," he said, "if you try to push it from behind, it just tangles and doubles back on itself. Soldiers have to be led from the front, not pushed from behind." Eisenhower may not have been colorful, but he could definitely get his point across in a way anyone could understand. He had character in the true sense.

The *fourth* point is that one of the biggest pitfalls for a charismatic leader comes straight from his or her ability to inspire love and devotion. In order to bask in the warm glow of a leader's approval, people may become reluctant to voice disagreements. There are people who become isolated because subordinates are afraid of it. But the same isolation can occur as the result of misplaced affection. People of character are usually well-loved by everyone around them. But they make it clear that their own first love is for the truth, even if it hurts.

Character and charisma are topics that have been defined and debated for thousands of years. I want to close this discussion with a comparison between two historical personalities.

Alexander the Great was undoubtedly the most charismatic leader who ever lived. He lived only to the age of thirty-three. He personally led his armies into one victorious battle after another. First in Greece, then Persia, then Egypt, and finally India. It wasn't always easy, however.

Alexander's willingness to put himself in danger, his gift for oratory, and his genius as a military tactician inspired fanatical loyalty from his troops. But even they grew weary after years of constant warfare. More than once they threatened to mutiny and returned to Greece. But until they reached the malaria-ridden jungles of India, Alexander was always able to rally them for one more battle. He believed that he was a god and that his wars of conquest demonstrated his divine power to the rest of the world. When he died in the ancient city of Babylon, his body was transported across the desert to Egypt in a golden hearse drawn by scores of horses.

Yet no one worships Alexander today. No one is impressed by all of the cities he named after himself, or by the city he named after his horse, or by the palace he built and filled with huge pieces of furniture so that people would think that he was a giant. In fact, Alexander's influence began to evaporate soon after his death. The remains of his empire were fought over by his generals, and new conquerors soon took his place.

Three hundred years after Alexander, Jesus Christ began to preach. Instead of an army, He had twelve men. Others tried to say that He was a god, but He never said so Himself; He didn't own a horse; He never founded a city; and when He died there was no golden hearse. Yet the force of His character has endured and grown—while the most charismatic leader who ever lived is of little interest to anyone except historians. Character is what is left after charisma is gone.

To elaborate a bit on a comparison I made earlier about how creating your character is like an artist creating a sculpture, the essential point is this: character is not something that happens by itself, any more than a chisel can create a work of art without the hand of an artist guiding it. In both instances, a conscious decision has been made; a conscious process of design is at work.

Character is the result of hundreds and hundreds of choices you may make that gradually turn who you are at any given moment into who you want to be. If that decision-making process is not present, you will still be somebody, you will still be alive—but you may have a personality rather than character. To me, that is something very different.

The United States has always been a country in which people have felt free to change themselves and the circumstances in which they live. In this regard, I happened to come across some interesting facts about the settlers who crossed the plains in covered wagons in the 1800s. For the most part, these people were neither recent arrivals on our shores nor were they facing any special economic difficulties. Instead,

Character is the result of your choices that turn you into who you want to be.

they were shopkeepers, farmers, and tradespeople who simply decided to make some big changes in their lives in the hope of finding something better despite all of the dangers and uncertainties.

No one really knows why this great migration began. But I suspect it had something to do with our fundamental belief in individual freedom. And the idea that if there is something better at the end of the rainbow, we have a responsibility to take advantage of it. That's the basis for our discussion of character in this book.

Character isn't something you were born with and can't change, like your fingerprints. It's something that you were *not* born with and you must take responsibility for making a good character part of who you are.

You may not be able to cross the Rocky Mountains in a covered wagon, but you can still create a better life for yourself by crossing the mountains of your soul. And that may be an even greater challenge.

There used to be a joke about football teams that lost every game. The coach would say to the team, "Well, we built a lot of character this year, didn't we?" That kind of character is what you settle for when you haven't achieved what you really wanted. Or as if character is something that automatically develops in you as a result of adversity. I don't buy that.

I don't think adversity by itself builds character. And I certainly don't think that success erodes it. You can build character by how you respond to what happens in your life. Whether it is winning every game or losing every game. Or getting rich or dealing with hard times.

You build character out of certain qualities that you must create and diligently nurture within yourself. Just like you would plant and water a seed or gather wood and build a campfire. You have to look for what is in your heart and your gut. You have to chisel away in order to find them. Just like chiseling away rock in order to create the sculpture that has previously existed only in your imagination.

The really amazing thing about character is that if you are sincerely committed to making yourself into the person you want to be, you will not only create those qualities, you'll strengthen them and recreate them in abundance, even as you are drawing on them every day of your life. Like the burning bush in the biblical book of Exodus[1]—the bush that burned but was not consumed by the flame—character sustains itself and nurtures itself, even as it is being put to work, ingested, and challenged.

COURAGE

The first unshakable and vital character trait is *courage*. As you take your metaphorical chisel in hand and set about discovering and creating the various qualities of character within yourself, you are going to need this one perhaps more than all of the others. Since ancient times, philosophers have seen courage as the basis of all real achievements.

There is a book that tells the stories of all of the winners of the Congressional Medal of Honor—it will bring tears to your eyes when you read it. It is one of the most powerful documents ever written. Stories of one American after another who put aside all thought of safety and faced down death in the service of their country. And more often than not, it has been in order to save other Americans rather than defeat an enemy. When you read of their exploits, you realize that these were people who simply lost their fear of death in order to do what had to be done.

Yes, those Medal of Honor winners were courageous individuals. But by itself, is overcoming the fear of death necessarily an expression of courage? I don't doubt that there are many people in this country who break the law and aren't afraid to die in the process. But I wouldn't call them courageous.

And there are people who do deliberately fool-hardy things with their cars that jeopardize their own lives and the lives of others. But they are not courageous people. In fact, a hungry donkey will keep eating until its stomach bursts; even if you hit him with a stick trying to make him stop. He has overcome his fear alright, but is obviously not courageous.

We may not be able to precisely define it, but we intuitively sense that there is some difference between acts of rashness and the accomplishment of those of the winners of the Congressional Medal of Honor. Let me sum up in a couple of sentences what those differences reveal about the true nature of courage. I can't put it any better than Greek philosopher Aristotle did more than two thousand years ago: "A truly courageous person is not someone who never feels fear. But who fears the right things at the right time in the right way."

What exactly does that mean? What does it mean to fear the right thing in the right way at the right time? To find the answer, let's look at some specific sources of fear that many individuals are facing right now. First, a great many people are afraid of what might happen to them financially. And it is certainly true that great changes are taking place in the economy that will have a direct impact on millions of people. I've heard it said that a corporation that employs ten thousand men and women today, may only need one-fifth that many within ten years.

Over the past fifty years, whole sections of our society have learned to identify with the corporation that employed them. That corporation provided not only a salary with health benefits, but also the opportunity to create a pension fund that would make retirement possible at age sixty-five or even sooner.

Now the relationship between the employer and the corporation is changing. Much of the work that used to be done by domestic workers can now be done more cheaply overseas. And companies are taking advantage of that. Perhaps out of necessity, perhaps simply to fatten the bottom line. In any case, the fear of losing one's job has reached segments of the workforce that have never faced it in quite this way.

What else are we afraid of? Many people are concerned about their health. They are afraid that they will get sick because they are not getting enough exercise. Or because they are eating the wrong thing. Or because of chemicals in the air or their food or water. In fact, I think people today are even more frightened of these things than they were in the past when epidemics of disease and poor sanitation were everywhere. And with regard to their health, people are also afraid of the expenses that might result if they were to become sick or disabled. Or the expenses that they would have to bear if this were to happen to a parent or a family member.

So, finance-related fears and health-related fears are two of our major concerns. But the third thing that I sense that really scares people today is a bit less easy to categorize. It is a general feeling that things aren't as good as they used to be. That there has been a loss of control at some basic level of our society. There is a sense that one earthquake after another, some large and obvious, some smaller and almost imperceptible, have accumulated to shift the foundations of society. And it is going to keep on shifting toward a result that is anything but good.

Keeping in mind our idea that a courageous person is not someone who never feels fear, but who fears the right thing at the right time in the right way, let's ask ourselves if these fears really fit that definition. I think that if we look a little deeper we'll see that what really scares people about these situations is that they are going to be helpless. That all of their trust was placed in somebody or something, and now they have been let down so that they can't do anything; they are helpless.

Refuse to feel helpless—there are always options.

But remember, you are never really helpless. And the sense that you are helpless, or that you might be if certain things were to happen, is something that we really ought to be afraid of. And that we should refuse to accept. You are never just the victim of circumstance. No matter what happens, you are never without options that can get you back on track. It takes courage to recognize that because it means accepting responsibility for your own future. But I would suggest that we should accept that responsibility because no one is really going to accept it for us; no matter what we may have been led to believe.

Let me emphasize that underlying most fears is the fear of helplessness, of being victimized or being blown around by the winds of fate like a leaf is blown off of a tree. But is that really a legitimate way of looking at things? To me, it sounds like being afraid of the dark. In which case, the best thing to do is to get yourself up, out of bed, and switch on the lights.

After all, the people who built this country didn't feel helpless when they faced obstacles that we can hardly even imagine today. I'm not saying we should all just gather around the campfire and tell stories about George Washington. But we should realize that every generation has faced insecurities, and lived with them, and triumphed over them. Only in the past fifty years or so is when people have come to expect a life without real tough times and real difficulties.

But adversity is not something to fear. It is something to expect, something to prepare for, and something to overcome.

Truly courageous people:

- Are not immune to fear; it plays a different role in their lives than it does for other people.

- Are not fearful about what someone might do to them or something might happen to them, their fears are about not living up to their ideals, about reacting instead of acting, about not taking advantage of the opportunities that are always within reach.

- Are not afraid of what might or might not happen next week or next year, they fear not making the most of every moment today.

- Fear the impulse to dominate other people; rather, they lead by helping others to be their best.

- Fear making appearances more important than reality; making impressions more important than communication; making themselves more important than those who are depending on them.

Expect, prepare for, and overcome adversity.

But there is one thing that a courageous person fears most. Have you ever seen a deer caught in the headlights of a car? The way the deer just stands there as though paralyzed as the car is bearing down? The truly courageous person fears getting caught like that. And a constant part of his or her life is dedicated to making sure that it never happens. In other words, the truly courageous person fears nothing except fear itself.[2]

NOTES

1. Exodus 3:2.

2. "There is nothing to fear but fear itself," Franklin D. Roosevelt, US President.

2

HONESTY
AND INTEGRITY

onesty and *integrity* are two qualities of a strong character that are fairly easy to define:

- Say what you mean, mean what you say. Do what you say you are going to do when you say you are going to do it. That is integrity.

- A clear correlation between words and deeds. Don't lie. Tell the truth. That is honesty.

Despite the fact that these are some of the clearest, most easily recognized elements of strong character, in the real world, honesty and integrity are some of the most difficult to find.

It seems that it has always been that way. In ancient Greece, the philosopher Demosthenes went searching for an honest man. He never found one. I have been fortunate; I think I have known a great many honest people. But if I measured that number against all of the less-than-ethical people I have encountered, I guess I would have to admit that even in my experience, honesty and integrity are rather rare. Why is that?

I hope to provide some answers. But just as our discussion with courage began with a look at fear; I want to start talking about honesty by looking at the exact opposite of honest behavior.

DISHONESTY

There was a time when telling a lie was very serious business. I'm speaking now of the days before lawsuits and legally enforceable contracts. In those days, lying was a very serious matter. It was also very serious if you accused someone of lying. Today a breach of integrity in a business matter might mean calling in the lawyers. But for hundreds of years in the past, calling someone a liar was the most common way to provoke a duel, at first with swords, later with pistols. Dishonesty was treated like a personal insult that demanded immediate redress. Everyone knew the big problems that could result if you got caught lying to another person. So, lying took a certain amount of...what is the right word? Foolish bravery, maybe.

But there is no such risk today, is there? Some people lie all of the time without thinking about it. Most people know when they are being lied to, which they may find irritating. But they just accept it. Maybe they decide to become liars themselves. In any case, very few duels are being fought.

To explain this, I think we can make a comparison between how some people today feel about lying and about how they feel about money. It used to be, you either had money or you didn't. When you bought something and the bill came, you had to pay it or there was an immediate problem. There were only two alternatives. You took care of your debts or you were a thief. Some people would literally take their own lives if they couldn't honor their debt. I am sure that we would agree that that is not exactly true any longer.

Many people don't feel the same kind of personal responsibility about paying debts promptly. And today, of course, we can put off paying for our purchases as long as we can make the minimum payment on our credit card. The pain that comes with having to shell out hard cash for something, the pain of maybe having to give up something in order to have something, we can now avoid that pain by putting it off indefinitely as plastic debt.

Of course, there is a high rate of interest on that debt, and the balance due can quickly mount up. But most people don't even think about that. It is the price they pay to have exactly what they want right now.

There are many situations where it is painful to tell the truth. It's painful in the same way, just as paying a big fat bill is painful. In fact, we even use the same words to talk about paying debts and telling the truth. We may talk about somebody's money is like "money in the bank." We talk about being "held accountable," about having to "account for yourself," about being called "to account."

If you have done something you are really not proud of and you are called to account for it, well, what does that feel like? How do you handle it? What are your options when you have to explain something that makes you uncomfortable? It's a bit like that moment of decision when the credit card bill comes every month. If you want to pay off the whole balance, there may be some pain and sacrifice involved. You may have to grit your teeth. You know that your life will be simpler in the long run, but it is going to hurt a little right now to pay off the new golf clubs or the new computer, or how about the sixty-foot yacht? I don't know if you can actually put a yacht on a credit card, but I have certainly known people who would if they could.

Gritting your teeth and paying in full can hurt. So quite often it seems easier to pay the minimum and delay the pain until next month. It's easier to float the truth of your finances off into a little imaginary flying carpet, and sail it into the mailbox. Of course, it's not really a flying carpet. It is more like a boomerang that is going to come around and hit you in the back of the head someday. But as Scarlett O'Hara said, "I'll think about that tomorrow." For the time being it is *Gone with the Wind*.

AVOIDING A BANKRUPT CHARACTER

Let me give you some good advice about avoiding a bankrupt character. Pay your ethical debt, keep your integrity in the black, face ugly realities with the truth as soon as they appear. When you feel that temptation to hedge, resist it immediately. Don't treat it casually. Treat it like a grease fire in the kitchen that you have to put out before it burns your house down or fills the place up with so much smoke that you can't see where you are going anymore. Because that is exactly what will happen when your ethical capital runs out. You won't be able to see where you are going anymore.

There is another way that being untruthful is like buying on credit—both are addictive. At first, they both go down so easily. They leave you wanting more. Any addictive behavior offers a simple short-term escape from a problem. But that escape becomes more and more complicated as time goes on.

Lying can get extremely complicated. You really have to have an outstanding memory to be a good liar, because you have to create more lies that are consistent with the one you told in the first place.

Many have been caught up in a dilemma like that. Shakespeare had it right all along, "What a tangled web we weave when, at first, we practice to deceive." Maybe you think I am being a bit tough here. Am I really saying that in every instance you have to tell the truth, the whole truth, and nothing but the truth?

So if somebody asks me, "How are you today?" I'm supposed to say, "Well, I have to be honest with you, I have a sore finger, last night I had a headache, and I've got to admit that my foot hurts a little." No, that's not what I mean. In fact, I think there are many times when some flexibility with the whole truth and nothing but the truth is called for. I will be discussing those later. Outright lying, however, planned lying, lying with an ulterior motive, lying for personal gain—that kind of lying should definitely be avoided.

UNTRUTHFULNESS

But untruthfulness is so tempting today and I want to make a clear distinction between what I call foolish lying, silly lying, or

29

stupid lying—and lying that is downright evil and poisonous to the character. Boasting, bombast, blarney, bragging, these are all the same thing. They are always floating around in the atmosphere. They can affect you at any time, like catching a cold. They are mostly harmless unless you start building a whole personality on them. Which has definitely happened to some people.

Some other guy scored the touchdown back in high school but you are watching the Super Bowl with your neighbor and you say that you did it. That is pretty harmless. You really don't know Joe, the president of XYZ Corporation; you were just introduced to him one time. But the client you are trying to impress has never even shaken hands with Joe. So here is a chance to score some points. That's pretty harmless, too. You are not really the creative director of your ad agency; you are the copywriter. But a woman sitting beside you on the plane to Phoenix will never know the difference. It is harmless. Unless she walks into your office someday, and it is a small world. But you will chance it; after all, it's just all hot air.

This is all going on that credit card mentioned a moment ago. There is such a thing as boasting in reverse, too. People who flaunt their frugality, people who "poor-mouth," people who are oppressively ostentatious in their lack of ostentation. This is actually becoming more common. Keep an eye out for it. All of this is childish trash talk. And it is usually spontaneous. It comes from succumbing to a moment of social pressure. It's not the kind of behavior that defines strong character.

But even strong characters have been known to indulge in it. Ernest Hemingway was a great writer and one of the most powerful personalities of the century. But he could be reckless, too. In any case, this kind of bragging and blarney should be distinguished from what I consider real lying.

Real lying isn't like putting bills on the credit card. Real lying is like theft. In my opinion, a key element in this kind of lying is the presence of planning and premeditation. If somebody is a supervisor in a corporation, and steals a subordinate's idea and takes credit for it in the eyes of the CEO, that requires a whole chain of events. And it is a conscious decision to keep the deception going through the various links in the chain. That kind of lying is theft.

That kind of lying is not only theft of the subordinate's idea, it's stealing from the CEO, too. It's stealing the CEO's sense of reality. It's creating an illusion. If someone falsifies an earning's report to inflate the price of a company's stock, that is deliberately creating a mirage in the minds of the investors. In the real world, both of these examples have happened. And many times, lives and careers have been ruined.

It's been my experience that those who engage in serious lying and unethical behavior get caught one way or the other. Usually the people being deceived awake from the illusions that have been foisted upon them. But even if this never happens. The criminal—and I don't think that is too strong of a word—has to buy into the illusion so deeply that his/her own sense of reality is eroded.

All of it—small-time lying and big-time deceit—comes from fear. Somebody is afraid that the truth about themselves isn't good enough. So they depart from the truth. Somebody secretly fears that they can't really come up with ideas of their own, so they steal somebody else's ideas. Or they fear that their company isn't really going to succeed, so they come up with a way to inflate the share prices. It is really cowardice.

Remember, courage is fearing the right thing, at the right time, and in the right way. *Fear* the temptation to misrepresent who you are, what you've done, or intend to do. *Trust* who you really are. *Trust* your ability to earn the respect of others. *Pay whatever price the truth costs.* Pay that bill immediately; because in the long run, it is a real bargain.

When you are in a leadership position, whether in a business or as the head of a family, honesty, and integrity are not as important as money or shelter or a phone. Honesty and integrity are infinitely more important than any of those things. They are about as important as having air, food, and water.

EVERYDAY WORLD REALITY

For a leader, honesty and integrity are absolutely essential to survival and success. A lot of business people don't realize how close they are being watched by their subordinates. Remember when you were a kid in grammar school? How you used to sit there staring at the teacher all day? By the end of the school year, I'll bet you could have done a perfect imitation of all your teacher's mannerisms. I'll bet you were aware of the slightest nuances in your teacher's voice. All of the little clues that distinguish levels of meaning, that told you the difference between bluster and *now I mean business.* You were able to do that after eight or nine months of observation.

Suppose you had five or ten years? Do you think there would have been anything about your teacher that you didn't know?

As a manager, there probably isn't anything that your people don't know about you right this minute. If you haven't been totally above board and honest with them, it's certain that you haven't gotten away with it. But if you have been led to believe that you have gotten away with it, it's most likely because people are afraid of you. That is a problem in its own right.

But there is another side of the coin, too. In any organization, people want to believe in their leaders. If you give them reason to trust you, they are not going to go looking for reasons to think otherwise. And they will be just as perceptive of your positive qualities as they are about the negative ones.

I heard a story that happened some time ago at a company in the Midwest. The wife of the new employee experienced complications in the delivery of a baby. There was a medical bill of more than ten thousand dollars. And the health insurance

By trying to loosen other people's grasp of the truth, you end up losing your own.

did not want to cover it—the employee hadn't been on the payroll long enough, the pregnancy was a pre-existing condition, one thing or another. In any case, the employee was desperate. He approached the company's CEO and asked him to talk to the insurance people. The CEO agreed. And the next thing the employee knew, the bill was gone. The charges were rescinded.

But when he mentioned to some of his colleagues the way the CEO had so readily used his influence with the insurance company, they just shook their heads and smiled. The CEO had paid the bill out of his own pocket and everybody knew it. No matter how quietly it had been done.

Equally, an act of dishonesty cannot be hidden. And it will instantly undermine the authority of a leader. But an act of integrity is just as obvious to all concerned. When you are in a leadership position, you have the choice of how you will be seen—and you *will* be seen one way or the other. Make no mistake about that.

FAMILY LEADERSHIP STANDARDS

The leadership of the family demands even higher standards of honesty and integrity. And the stakes are higher, too. You can replace disgruntled employees and start over. You can even get a new job for yourself if it comes to that. But your family can not be shuffled like a deck of cards.

If you haven't noticed, kids are great moral philosophers. Especially as they enter adolescence. They are determined to discover and expose any kind of hypocrisy, phoniness, or lack of integrity on the part of the authority figure. And if we are parents, that means us. It is frightening how unforgiving kids can be about this. But it isn't really a conscious decision on their part. It is just a necessary phase of growing up. They are testing everything, especially parents.

In Arthur Miller's great play *Death of a Salesman,* it's hard to believe that a son would so completely lose faith in his father, based on a single instance of dishonesty. Once a parent has lost moral authority, it is very, very difficult to regain it.

Studies have shown that children are extremely understanding about many things. For example, if you accidentally step on a favorite toy, that will quickly be forgiven if not forgotten. If you lose your job and the family has to move, they will adjust. If parents just can't get along and decide to divorce, most kids can handle it. But they can't handle dishonesty. It can take many, many years before that will be forgiven.

People keep pictures of their kids on their desks or in their wallets. Is it to remind them what they look like? Is it to show them off to people? Perhaps. But there is an even more important reason people keep their children's pictures close by—to remind us of what is at stake when we make decisions that determine character. And we all make many of those decisions, every day.

As a person of integrity yourself, you'll find it easy to teach integrity to your kids. And they in turn will find it easy to accept you as a teacher. This is a great opportunity and also a supreme responsibility. Kids simply must be taught to tell the truth—to mean what they say and to say what they mean.

There was something interesting about the Native American peoples of the southwest in times gone by and the skills they felt were important for their children to know. Hiding was one of them. In a desert environment you would think there was no place to hide, except possibly by squeezing behind a cactus plant—yet the children could literally disappear. And running was another very important ability. Beginning as young as six or seven years of age, children were taught to run long distances while holding a mouthful of water, to develop breath control. And, of course, both running and hiding were skills that could save a child's life as well as preserve the security of the group.

Kids today must also be taught skills that will save their lives. And integrity is one of those vitally important skills. Maybe it's hard to convince yourself of that.

I heard a story of a man who flew propeller-driven antisubmarine planes for the Navy. He piloted them on long flights over the water. He told of an incident where a storm was coming, and they were faced with a difficult navigational problem to avoid it. It became even more difficult when the navigator revealed that he couldn't handle it. He cheated his way through some parts of the training—training material that didn't seem very useful.

I can't promise that integrity will ever save their lives, but nothing you will ever do is more important than living integrity in front of your children, and teaching them the same. There is an old saying, "Those who can, do; and those who can't, teach." But you really can't teach honesty unless you are honest yourself. You really can't teach integrity unless you also live with integrity. It's actually quite simple.

MORE HONEST THAN WISE

Earlier I suggested that there may be times when a certain amount of flexibility with the truth is appropriate. I'd like to return to that now. It might be tempting, for the sake of consistency, to assert that you should always tell the whole truth exactly as you see it in every situation. But I've lived long enough in the real world to know that things just aren't that simple. Shakespeare wrote of one of his characters, "Every man has his faults, and honesty is his. He is more honest than wise."

Just as there is a difference between blowing hot air and premeditated dishonesty, there is also a difference between lying and recognizing the differences of diplomacy. How can you tell the difference? Your gut feelings will tell you. By the time we reach adulthood, I think most people have extremely accurate ethical barometers built into our heads and hearts. We may choose to ignore what that ethical barometer tells us, but it's there nonetheless.

When you are in a leadership role—whether in the work-place or at home—I believe there is at least one situation in which you are almost always justified in stretching the truth to some degree. And here it is—you should overstate your degree of enthusiasm for your employees and/or family. Use many, many carrots and very few sticks. Your recipe for being with others should include at least three parts praise for every one part of criticism.

Will this stretching of the truth cost you respect? I don't think so. Will a little sugar-coating of your true feelings foster greater productivity, better work, improved morale, and better relationships? Absolutely! And that conclusion is supported by a great deal of behavioral science research. Praise is one of the world's most teaching and leadership tools. Criticism and blame, even if deserved, are counter-productive unless all other approaches have failed.

Vince Lombardi, the late coach of the Green Bay Packers, certainly deserved his reputation as a tough manager and a man of strong character. But even he knew the importance of building up people's egos. You could have seen how this worked if you had the opportunity to attend a practice session of the Packers during the years when they were one of the most powerful football teams ever assembled.

Lombardi had a quarterback from his scout team throwing passes against the first-string defense. And this young quarterback was obviously eager to impress the coach. But after the player had completed three or four passes in a

Recipe for success: three parts praise for every one part criticism.

row, Lombardi seemed anything but impressed. In fact, he seemed quite displeased.

He took the scrubbed quarterback aside. "What are you trying to do, wreck my team?" Lombardi snarled. "Start throwing interceptions..." and you had better believe he started throwing them. You can call it diplomacy, psychology, or just plain flattery. But it often brings out the best in people. It is the grease that keeps the machine of human interaction functioning smoothly. So, honesty is the best policy. But sometimes even a little less than total honesty is even better.

SELF-HONESTY

We've been talking mostly about the importance of honesty and integrity in dealing with other people. But I want to conclude now by focusing on what those qualities mean with your relationship with yourself. I think a term from clinical psychology is useful here—*cognitive dissonance*. I'll use a quick example to illustrate what it means. Let's consider a man who is an expert on personal financial planning. He makes a good living advising people about life insurance, trust funds, and the various kinds of mortgages. But a great deal of his business is devoted to helping individuals who are deeply in debt. Who need to tear up their credit cards and start saving instead of spending. Sometimes there is no alternative but to declare bankruptcy and start over.

We are so surprised when one day, this expert on personal financial planning says that he is going out of business. "I just can't take the pressure anymore. It's too much stress." Well, we can understand that. It must be stressful facing the problems of one person after another who is in trouble financially. To work through it with them day in and day out. But here is the big surprise. "I'm the one who is in trouble financially," he admits. "I'm behind on everything. Even my car payment. And after lecturing about the perils of debt all day, I can't stand to look in the mirror anymore."

Wow! This man is experiencing cognitive dissonance in an extreme form. He is trying to live with two conflicting images of himself in his head. And the strain is simply using up all of his energy. He is fundamentally a good person; he really believes in doing the right thing. But that is the trouble. He knows he is living a lie. And the stress of that finally gets to him.

You might be surprised by the percentage of high-level managers and professional people who secretly know that they are presenting a false image to the world. The need to keep up appearances. The competition with peers. The pressure to make every year better than the last one. All this makes it very tempting to put on a mask. I'm not talking about just boasting here. I'm talking about creating a real split between what you are telling the world and what you know is the real truth about yourself.

Another Shakespeare quote, "All the world is a stage...," and to some extent, we are all playing roles. But living with honesty and integrity can make life a great deal easier to live. This is where ethics and psychology really overlap. Not only is it right to minimize cognitive dissonance, but in the long run it is also a lot easier on your psyche.

We all know people who got ahead as a result of dishonest or unethical behavior. When you are a kid, you think that never happens. But when you get older, you realize that it does—you see the long-term consequences of dishonest gain and you realize that it doesn't pay in the end. I have seen people who have made millions with questionable business tactics. And I have also seen a higher percentage of health problems among those people than any insurance actuary could possibly account for.

I've seen people who decided to sell out their friends or their business partners in order to cash a big check. And those people end up looking twenty years older than their age. Stick around, keep your eyes open, and I think you will see it's true.

"Hope of dishonest gain is the beginning of loss" is another old saying I believe is true. I don't think it refers to the loss of money. I think it means the loss of self-respect. You can have all the material things in the world, but if you have lost respect for yourself, what do you really have? The only way to ever attain success and enjoy it is to receive it honestly and with pride in what you have done. Hey, that's not just a sermon, that is very practical advice. You can not only take it to heart, but you can also take it to the bank.

3

PERSEVERANCE

Someone told me of a man who raises thoroughbred racehorses. And one of his favorite words is "class." He talks about how one horse has class and another one doesn't—and how this class can make a difference in a race. That's a little puzzling to me. Because it seems like the horse that could run fastest would win, whether it has class or not. So what did he mean by the word "class"?

According to this man, class is calling on reserve energy. Class is the ability to overcome any number of challenges in a race. Class doesn't mean that you never get tired—but it does mean you never show it. Class doesn't mean that you are not tempted to quit sometimes—but it does mean that you never actually do. And in the final yards of a race, class makes the difference.

The title of this chapter is *Perseverance*. But it could very well have been *Class,* because they seem to be very similar qualities. Whatever word you want to use, this is an extremely important element of strong character. I also suspect that in recent years we have overlooked the importance of perseverance to some extent, because we believe so strongly in talent as the true determinant of success.

For instance, there are a great many special programs in the schools for so-called "gifted children." These programs can begin as early as the first grade. A child is tested and is either gifted or not. The child either has talent or not. Our expectations of this child change based on the results of certain tests—and the child's expectations of him or herself also change.

Of course, there are some educational systems that place a little less faith in talent, and a little more faith in long-hard work. And those systems are the source of some incredible progress in recent years. I think it is important to look closely at perseverance—no matter what your gifts and talents may be.

DEVELOPING PERSEVERANCE

Can you develop perseverance? After all, that quality is something bred into racehorses over many generations. Can the human equivalent of class and perseverance really be learned the way you can learn to drive a car or play a musical instrument? To a great extent, I think yes, perseverance can be learned. And there are some very powerful techniques that can help you learn it.

By far, the most important tool you can use in developing perseverance is a personal list of challenging, realistic, well-defined, and highly-rewarding goals. Goals are major to a genuinely success-oriented person. Without goals, you are just playing around. The difference between a goal-directed individual and someone without goals is like the difference between a Wimbledon champion and a kid batting a tennis ball around on a court with no net, no opponent to bring out the best, and no way of keeping score.

Despite everything that has been written about the importance of goal setting, very few people put it into practice. It has always amazed me how the average person puts more thought and effort into planning a two-week vacation than devoting time to planning his or her life. What are they taking a vacation from? They haven't really decided what to do in life. But for two weeks out of the year, they decide that they want to do something else. And this is what they plan very carefully—a vacation.

EFFECTIVE GOAL SETTING

Challenge creates strong character. Goals represent challenges in their most positive form. Leaders have their personal goals clearly in focus. As well as the goals of the organization and/or family. In fact, one of the principal responsibilities of leadership is defining goals for the vast majority of people who are unable to do it for themselves. Over the years I have developed ideas about effective goal setting that I share throughout this book. I also point out some traps of goal-directed behavior that are not usually talked about, but they certainly ought to be.

When I was a kid, I used to dream of what it would be like to buy a ticket on a railroad train and just go someplace. I really didn't think about where I'd be going or how I would get there, I just loved the idea of getting on the train and just letting it take me someplace. There is still something appealing about that idea—but it is certainly not the way to live your life as a mature human being.

When you grow up, you buy a ticket for a train or a plane because you want to go someplace, and you know exactly where you are going. You may have to change planes in a different city, your flight may be canceled, and you may have to switch to another flight. You may not feel like talking to the person next to you. But you will persist. You know where you are headed and you are quite determined to get there. That is goal-directed behavior in its simplest form.

There are short-term goals and long-term goals. Sometimes you are flying across the country, other times you are just walking down to the corner grocery store. Long-term goals are the equivalent of a major journey. When you reach the point where you have achieved your long-term goal, your life will be fundamentally changed. And the process of getting to that point will transform you into a stronger, wiser, higher-performing person than you are now.

How can you identify your long-term goals? On a sheet of paper or in a notebook, write these five headings:

1. What do I want to do?

2. What do I want to be?

3. What do I want to see?

4. What do I want to have?

5. Where do I want to go?

Now, under each of these categories, write down several possible long-term goals. Be very relaxed about this. Just allow your mind to flow, and come up with three to six ideas for each category. Don't worry about a lot of detail at this point. And don't spend too much time describing a particular goal.

In category number one, for example, *What do I want to do?* Suppose you want to write a book about the history of your family. Going back to the arrival of your great-grandparents in the United States. Just quickly jot down *family history.* Then as you look down at the list of categories, it occurs to you that you have always wanted to see the pyramids in Egypt. So you write *pyramids.* Keep writing down ideas as long as the list of categories continues to inspire you.

You will probably be surprised at the things that turn up. You may have kept a great many desires and aspirations hidden in the back of your mind. But the opportunity to write them down will move them to the forefront of your consciousness. That is one of the benefits of this technique.

When you are satisfied with your list of long-term goals, read through the list once again. Then, beside each item, write the number of years it will take you to achieve that particular goal. It is best to round off the number into one-year, three-year, five-year, and ten-year categories. For example, you may estimate that it will take you ten years to research and write the book on your family history. But you will need only five years to get yourself into the position to go to the pyramids. Create a time frame like this for each of your long-term goals.

Immediate goals will take less than a year to achieve are important, too, of course. And we will deal with those separately in a moment.

When you are finished entering your time frame, there should be a fairly balanced distribution of all your goals. If there are many one- and three-year objectives, but only a few in the ten-year category, maybe you need to think more about what you really want your life to add up to. What kind of life do you really want to build over the long run?

But if there is a preponderance of ten-year goals, and relatively few of the shorter-term variety, this may indicate that you are putting things off. That you are focused too much on the future and not enough on what you can accomplish right now. Keep working on your list. Adding and subtracting your goals with various time frames until you have created a more or less even distribution.

PRIORITIZING GOALS

Now comes the really challenging and interesting part. So far you have just been adding things to the list. But now it is time to start making some selections. Start asking yourself, *What is really important compared to what might just be sort of fun?* Choose four goals from each of the four time frames: one-year, three-year, five-year, and ten-year. Now you have sixteen separate goals that you have only referred to in a brief fashion.

But now you are going to start seeing each very clearly in your mind's eye. You are going to see each goal just as if it were being realized this very minute. And you are going to write down a detailed description of exactly what you see.

Do you intend to open a handmade furniture store in three years? What will the store look like from the street out front? Will there be gold-leafed lettering on the windows? Or will there be a sign hanging over the door instead? How many square feet will the store contain? Will there be a showroom area for the furniture in front and a workspace in the back? Or will the furniture be built at a different location? Do you intend to have employees or will you run the business entirely by yourself?

Think of all the questions that need to be answered with absolute clarity. And then write the information down in a notebook—which will become one of your most important personal possessions.

THE REASON FOR THE GOAL

But that's not all. Any goal is a powerful motivator *only if* there is a powerful reason behind it. Why do you want to achieve your goal? Why do you want to own a handmade furniture store? Or a private airplane? Or a newspaper in a small town in Vermont? Why do you want to compete in a triathlon? Or visit the Australian Outback? Or be the first person in your family to earn a PhD?

Write down your reasons for wanting these goals in the same degree of detail that you used to write your description. If you can't find a clear and convincing reason for each of your sixteen goals, do some serious re-evaluation. You may have more whim or pipedreams than real goals. And now is the time to make that discovery.

Keep working on your list until you have sixteen clearly envisioned, strongly motivating long-term goals. Regularly review what you have written, keeping track of your progress toward the objectives. Above all, *persevere*. Goal setting is a very important first step, but goal *achievement* is a continuous life-long process. That is what makes it so challenging. That is why it is also so extremely rewarding to finally attain your long-term goals.

With regard to *immediate goals,* those that require anywhere from a day to a year to achieve, I recommend

Perseverance is as important to goal achievement as gasoline is to a car.

creating lots of objectives that can be accomplished in a month or less. Write them down. Read what you have written at frequent intervals. Keep track of your progress. And do something often that brings you closer to realizing these very short-term objectives. That way you will always have something to celebrate. These goals are not only important in their own right, but they are also confidence builders and motivators toward a lifestyle based on perseverance and achievement.

Let me close this discussion by emphasizing the fundamental importance of goal setting for success, leadership, and creating a strong character. Let me also emphasize the fact that perseverance is about as important to goal achievement as gasoline is to driving a car. Sure there will be times when you feel like you are spinning your wheels, but you will also get out of the rut with genuine perseverance. Without it, you won't even be able to start your engine. That situation and how to avoid it is our next topic of discussion.

PROCRASTINATION

The opposite of perseverance is procrastination. Perseverance means you never quit. Procrastination usually means you never get started. I consider the inability to finish something to be a form of procrastination. Ask people why they procrastinate, and you'll often hear something like, "I'm a perfectionist. Everything has to be just right before I can get down to work. No distraction, not too much noise, no telephone calls interrupting me. And of course, I have to be feeling well physically, too. I can't work when I have a headache."

The other end of procrastination, being unable to finish, also has a perfectionistic explanation. "I'm just never satisfied. I'm my own harshest critic. If all the i's aren't dotted, and all the t's aren't crossed, I just can't consider that I am done. That is just the way I am. And I'll probably never change."

Do you see what's going on here? A fault is being turned into a virtue. The perfectionist says that his or her standards are just too high for this world. This fault-into-virtue syndrome is a common defense when people are called upon to discuss their weaknesses. But in the end, it is just a very pious kind of excuse-making. It certainly doesn't have anything to do with what is really behind procrastination.

The basis of procrastination could be, "Fear of failure." That is what extreme perfectionism really is once you take a hard look at it. What is the difference whether you are afraid of being less than perfect, or being afraid of anything else?

You are still paralyzed by fear. What is the difference if you never start or never finish? You are still stuck. You are still going nowhere. You are still overwhelmed by whatever task that is before you. You are still allowing yourself to be dominated by a negative vision of the future in which you see yourself being criticized, laughed at, punished, or dismissed. Of course this negative version of the future is really a mechanism that allows you to do nothing. It's a very convenient mental tool.

I'm going to tell you specifically how to overcome procrastination. I'm going to show you how to turn procrastination into perseverance. And if you do what I suggest, the process will be virtually painless. If you have been using a negative vision of the future as a mental tool or inactivity, I'm going to ask you to toss it aside and start using two other very powerful principles that foster productivity and perseverance instead of passivity and procrastination. The two principles: 1) break it down; 2) write it down.

BREAK IT DOWN

The first principle is *break it down*. No matter what you are trying to accomplish, whether it is writing a book, climbing a mountain, or painting a house, the key to achievement is your ability to break down the tasks into manageable pieces and knock them off one at a time. Focus on accomplishing what is right in front of you at this moment. Ignore what is off in the distance. Substitute real-time positive thinking for negative future visualization. That's the first all-important technique for bringing an end to procrastination.

Suppose I were to ask you if you could write a four-hundred-page novel. If you are like most people, that would be an impossible task. As soon as I ask you that question, a picture appears in your mind of a big fat book lying on a coffee table with hundreds and hundreds of words covering every page. Yet, somebody must have written the book that you see in your mind's eye. But that person surely wasn't you. Suppose I ask you a different question, "Do you think you could write a page and a quarter a day, for one year." Do you think that you could do it? Now the task is starting to seem more manageable. We are breaking down the four-hundred-page book into bite-size pieces. But even so, many people would still find the prospect intimidating.

Why? Writing a page and a quarter may not seem so bad, but you're being asked to look ahead one whole year. When people start to look that far ahead, many go into a negative mode. So let me formulate the idea of writing a book in yet another way. Let me break it down even more.

Suppose I were to ask you, "Can you fill up a page and a quarter...not for a year, not for a month, not even for a week...just today?" Don't look any further ahead than that. I believe that most people would confidently declare that they could accomplish that. And of course, these people are the same people who feel totally incapable of writing a whole book.

Then if I said the same thing to those people tomorrow. If I told them, "I don't want you to look back, I don't want you to look ahead, I just want you to fill up a page and a quarter this day. Do you think you can do it?" You have probably heard the phrase, "Take one day at a time," that is what we are doing here. We are breaking down the time required for a major task into one-day segments. And we are breaking down the work involved in writing a four-hundred-page book into one page and a quarter increments. Keep this up for one year and you will write the book.

Discipline yourself to look neither forward nor backward and you can accomplish things that you never thought you could possibly do. One of the beauties of this technique is that you can really take it to the extremes if you have to. If writing a page and a quarter in one day still seems too much for you, break it down even more. Try to write three sentences in the next hour. Don't look any further ahead than that. Come up with a way of looking at the task to finally seem manageable. Then all you have to do is persevere. Procrastination won't be a problem because the task will now be so small that fear won't kick in. And it all begins with those three words: *break it down.*

WRITE IT DOWN

My second technique for defeating procrastination is also only three words long: *write it down.* We have seen how important writing is to goal setting. The writing you do for beating procrastination is very similar. But instead of focusing on the future, you are now writing about the present. Just as you experience it every day. Instead of describing the things you want to do or the places you want to go, you're describing what you actually do with your time. And you are going to keep a written record of the places you actually go.

In other words, you are going to keep a diary of your activity. You will be amazed by the distractions, detours, and downright waste of time that you record during the course of the day. All of which hinder you from achieving your goals. For many people, it almost seems they plan it that way. And maybe, at some unconscious level, they do. The great thing about keeping a time diary is that it brings all hinderances out in the open. It forces you to actually see what you *are* doing and what you *aren't* doing.

The time diary doesn't have to be anything elaborate. Just buy a little spiral notebook that you can easily carry in your pocket or set up a file on your phone. When you go to lunch, when you drive across town, when you go to the dry cleaners, when you spend time shooting the breeze at the copy machine or in the break room, make a quick note of the time you began the activity and the time it ended. Try to make this notation as soon as possible. But if it is inconvenient to do it immediately, do it later. If possible, make an entry in your time diary at least once every thirty minutes. Do so for at least a week.

What else do you have to do to gain the benefits of this extremely powerful productivity technique? Nothing. You don't have to do anything else at all. It is just a process for making yourself aware of how you actually spend your time. You will naturally and effortlessly begin to reorganize your life. Perhaps that seems like too much to believe, but it's true.

When you are forced to write down the fact that you hung out at the copy machine for fifteen minutes today, you'll think twice about doing that again tomorrow. When you put it in writing that you worked on an important project for thirty minutes today and then took a break to read the newspaper, you will persevere a little longer on the project tomorrow and forget about the newspaper.

Keeping a diary for even one week can revolutionize your ability to focus and achieve your goals. Break it down, write it down—very easy to understand, very straightforward. Yet these are two powerful and effective productivity techniques that can put an end to procrastination. This is how you get yourself started.

But how do you keep going? How do you keep your motivation consistently high? How do you learn to persevere when the novelty has worn off and you are still some distance from your goal? Keep reading to find out.

PERSISTENT MOTIVATION

The Irish poet William Butler Yeats wrote a poem describing some of the unfortunate characteristics of the modern world. One of the things Yeats noticed is the fact that bad people seem to have the most energy—while good people become discouraged and doubtful of their own abilities. The best lack all convictions while the worst are filled with a passionate intensity. Those are the words Yeats used.

And it is true that we can look around the world and see all sorts of things happening that we might wish were not happening. And there are people working very hard to make those things happen for reasons that we might not admire. And when we see that, it is easy to start saying, "What's the use? What hope do I really have? Why don't I just give up on all of the things that I have been trying to accomplish and just start taking it easy?"

OTHER THAN YOURSELF

Even people of strong character feel that way sometimes. All of us have moments like that. That is when perseverance gets really, really tough. What is the answer? Well, recall that during our discussion of goal setting, I asked you to list five categories for your long-term goals: 1)What do you want to do? 2) What do you want to be? 3) What do you want to see? 4) What do you want to have? 5) Where do you want to go?

Now I want you to add another one: 6) With whom do you want to share? In other words, who are you working for besides yourself?

In the first five categories, you were asked to focus exclusively on your own aspirations and why they were important to you. But now, I want you to think in terms of other people. Ask yourself:

- Who is depending on you?
- Who will benefit if you persevere and succeed?
- Who will suffer if you give up and stop trying?
- Who can you reach out to when you have achieved your goals?

Write down answers to these questions, just like you wrote answers for the other categories.

For many people, the answers will appear quite readily. If you have a family, your spouse and your children are depending on you. Perhaps even your parents are depending on you now if they are elderly and require some care. But even if you are a single person or just starting out in your career, you can think of reasons to persevere and succeed that go beyond your personal needs.

Maybe you would like to share some of your financial success with the school that educated you, or with the religious institutions that gave you spiritual guidance, or with a hospital that helped to heal you on some occasions. This sharing doesn't have to be limited to money either. If your work has given you certain skills, you can share your time and your ability. You can and you should. But even this isn't putting it strongly enough.

It isn't just that you'll do better if you feel you are working for others in addition to yourself. You absolutely must find reason outside yourself to persevere if you want to keep going when the going gets tough. Ernest Hemingway wrote, "A man alone hasn't got a chance." And that doesn't mean only that you need people to help *you* in life, it means *you need to help other people*. You need people who can become the real reason for perseverance above and beyond your material possessions or your financial success. *What's in it for me,* can only take you so far. *What's in it for somebody besides me,* can take you as far as you need to go.

In the last days of World War II, the American cruiser Indianapolis was sunk by an enemy submarine. This was one of the most tragic incidents of the war for American forces, in which hundreds of men lost their lives. Many who made it through the initial attack had to spend days and nights in the water before rescuers arrived. The experience of trying to stay alive in the water was so overwhelming that many people simply gave up.

In fact, the survivors reported later that virtually everyone wanted to give up at one time or another. But whenever

Find a reason outside yourself to persevere, to keep going when the going gets tough.

someone wanted to quit trying, the others would talk to him about the people back home who needed him, who were depending on him to survive. And if there was no one depending on him right then, they would talk about people in the future who would someday be needing him. People he hadn't met yet, people who hadn't even been born yet. They conjured up all sorts of reasons above and beyond simply surviving.

This motivation beyond the self was the only motivation that was strong enough. And what was true in an extreme sense for those men in wartime, is also true in all of our lives. No matter what we are trying to accomplish.

We began this discussion with mentioning racehorses and how the best of them could overcome any challenge in a race. I don't know what motivates a racehorse. Whether it is a bale of hay just beyond the finish line or the thought of resting in a warm stall. But I doubt that there is much thought of what he can do for the other horses. Well, that's one big difference between horses and people. People depend on one another. And people of strong character take pride in what they can do for others.

Challenge yourself to *become a person who will have the strength to persevere.*

4

WISDOM

People are born hungry. During the first few moments of life, a human infant is totally consumed by its appetite. First for air, then for nourishment. People stay hungry; we're hungry all of our lives. But exactly what it takes to satisfy our hunger usually changes a great deal. By the time we reach adulthood, some of us are hungry for wealth and power. Some of us are hungry for truth. Some people want everyone to love them. Others want everyone to fear them.

But there is a fundamental challenge with all of our appetites—none of them can ever be permanently satisfied. When it comes to wanting things, there's no such thing as enough, which can really get on our nerves. For example, you buy a new car, but in a couple of years it's an old car. You get a new computer and it does everything really fast, faster than your neighbor's; but then a year goes by and now your neighbor gets a computer that is even faster than yours. Where does it all end?

There is really only one kind of person who is actually comfortable with the impossibility of satisfying their appetites. This person wants that mysterious commodity called *wisdom*, and wants it more than all the cars and computers in the world. Wisdom, like the learning capacity of the human brain, is infinite. There will always be more to know. And there will always be plenty of room in your brain for everything you learn. Life is really a paradise if you are someone who genuinely wants wisdom.

We all want to be successful, and I'm certainly in favor of that. But I have known some people who literally wanted all of the money they could get—not what the money could buy, but the money itself, the nickels, the dimes, the quarters. Wanting all of the money in the world is like wanting to know all there is to know in the world. Except the person who wants all of the money is miserable. He will never get it all, and he will never think he has enough. Even if he had rooms filled with thousand-dollar bills, he'd still want the next man's nickel. And he would be in pain about that. Filled with envy about it.

The person who wants wisdom also wants to look back over his shoulder at the other guy. But he just wants to see what the other guy is reading. And if the other guy is reading a book he hasn't read yet, he looks forward to reading it himself. The acquisition of wisdom is not what all the mathematicians call a zero-sum game; you don't have to give up something in order for me to have it. You can give me your wisdom, and now I'll have it. But you still have it, too. When one person shares wisdom with another, neither person is diminished. In fact, both are made wiser.

Giving and taking is such a basic experience for most of us. But the whole concept of giving and taking doesn't really apply to wisdom. There is no giving and taking, there is only sharing.

Wisdom is a unique commodity; if, indeed, it can even be called a commodity. Unlike the other things that others hunger for, wisdom is very hard to visualize. We could imagine rooms full of money, but how can you picture a room full of wisdom? Books aren't wisdom, they are just pieces of paper bound together. Books can help create wisdom in people's minds. But if you look inside their head, you won't find any wisdom there.

So, what is wisdom anyway?

To most people, wisdom seems like something in a distant country, as if it were on a tropical island somewhere. Few people, if any, have ever seen it. But it is something that everybody has heard reports about. Almost everybody believes wisdom exists, even if they have never seen it.

In that sense, wisdom is almost like God. Except it isn't a divine quality, it is a human quality. A very rare, very precious human quality. Ask anybody and they will probably tell you that there is such a thing as wisdom. Furthermore, that person will also tell you that he or she hopes someday to become wise. Ask the same person how to become wise, how to get wisdom. If that person has some wisdom, the person will probably just smile, nod, or tell you to live and look around you and think about what you see and hear.

LIVE AND LEARN

There was once a man who was a great investment banker. One of the foremost in the world in his profession. He was born in poverty in Europe. Was completely self-taught. He had used brains and guts to make a tremendous fortune. Many listened in fascination to this man telling the story of his life. And then someone would say, "Sir, you should write a book that sums up all you have learned about the world and how to succeed in it."

But this great international investment banker just looked and smiled. He said, "Well, I suppose I could do that. But it wouldn't, really, be much of a book. In fact, I could tell you everything I know in just fifteen or twenty minutes. Everything I have come to understand over the course of a lifetime. But what good would it do? These aren't things you can just hear about from someone else, or read in a book. Until you have discovered them for yourselves, they are just words, just puffs of air, or drops of ink on a page. You have to live in order to learn what I've learned. You have to arrive at these truths the way you arrive at your destination after a long journey, with that same sense of fulfillment and joy."

It's ironic, isn't it? Wisdom is not a thing that you can buy or a course you can take in a school or a degree you can earn. Yet, all parents want their children to attend good schools, and rightfully so. Wisdom is not really something you can get from another person. Yet, you can gain some wisdom from everyone you meet. Wisdom is something wise people always feel they need more of. Yet the true sources of wisdom lie nowhere but within ourselves.

There are many people who are too smart for their own good. People who are filled to overflowing with facts and technical knowledge, but who are sadly lacking in human understanding and common sense. We've all met people like that. They score high on all the tests. They get perfect grades in school. They win all prizes. They often get paid very well to practice their skills; to build things, to write computer programs, to carry on lawsuits, to manage other people's affairs.

The true source of wisdom lies within yourself.

But go home with one of these wizzes, look at their lives outside of work, if they have a life outside their work, and you will find that all sorts of things that regular people know like the difference between right and wrong and what's fair and how to give happiness and what life is worth, those really important aspects in life...they haven't even thought about.

REAL-WORLD WISDOM

"What has that got to do with me?" the smart one asks. "What is this thing you call common sense? What is this stuff you call human wisdom? What is this thing you call strong character?" I've seen people who have everything you could possibly want, every object you could dream of, everything you can drive down the street, sail on the ocean, or fly through the air—but on the inside, where the real person lives, they're broke, they have nothing. They haven't got a clue.

The Bible tells us that King Solomon was the wisest man in the whole world. He was not only the wisest, he was also the richest man in the world. Kings and queens came from all over to get Solomon's advice and to admire his riches. In fact, legend has it that Solomon had wives from every nation on earth. And there is no report of any marital disarmament, not one divorce. Was this a wise man or what?

The Bible tells us that when Solomon was just a young man, living in the courts of King David, his father, God told Solomon that He would grant him one wish. Do you know what he wished for? He didn't wish for a kingdom or great power or good looks or unlimited pleasure or long life or love or fame or security. Solomon asked God to grant him wisdom. And because he asked for wisdom and nothing else, God gave him wisdom and everything else, too.

The most important difference between you, me, and Solomon isn't where or when we were born. Or the privileges we have or don't. The difference isn't in our names or our bank accounts, or the positions we hold in life. The difference is Solomon got wisdom by asking God for it. The rest of us must look around for wisdom. And look for it in everything we read, do, and in everyone we meet. And most of all, we must look for it in ourselves. Perhaps more than any other element of strong character. Wisdom is a quality that we must earn and learn on our own.

Yes, wisdom is a unique component of character. If you don't have it, nobody can tell you what it is. And if you do have it, probably you will be wise enough never to say, "I am a wise person."

SOCRATES THE PHILOSOPHER

The wisest man in ancient Greece, the greatest philosopher the world has ever known, was a man named Socrates. In fact, Socrates made wisdom his profession. *Philosopher means lover of wisdom* in ancient Greek. Because he didn't have another job, I can imagine people were always asking him, "So what do you do for a living?"

He was definitely smart enough to figure out that he had to have an answer, so he made up his own job title, philosopher. But when people asked Socrates what is wisdom? He always gave the same answer. In fact, Socrates never claimed to know much of anything except how to know how to ask questions. And by asking questions, he would prove to other people that they didn't know what they thought they knew or were certain of.

Everybody in Greece agreed that Socrates was the wisest man in Greece. But unlike King Solomon, the philosopher Socrates didn't have great wealth. The wisest man in Greece was poor. King Solomon managed to run a huge household with many wives and homes and lots of children. And he accomplished this without any discord or unhappiness.

But Socrates had no home life at all. The wisest man in Greece was married to a famous and terrible nag; they had no children. Socrates, the wisest man in Greece, went to the marketplace every day and hung around and asked people questions. And he hoped to get invited to a banquet so he wouldn't have to go home and face his wife.

King Solomon was honored by all of the great leaders of his time; but Socrates, the wisest man in Greece, didn't even have any support among the powerful people in his country. Their sons would go to Socrates and learn what they could from the philosopher. But the powerful families of Athens, the Greek city where Socrates lived, got tired of Socrates' questions. They grew exasperated with the way he was teaching the youth of Greece; that nobody knows anything for sure. So they accused the wisest man in Greece of corrupting their children.

Instead of honoring the greatest philosopher who ever lived, the Athenians sentenced Socrates to death—unless he would take back what he thought and apologize. But Socrates didn't take it back; he didn't apologize. Socrates cheerfully drank down a cup of poison and just sat there calmly saying goodbye to his few faithful students who were asking questions the whole time.

Solomon and Socrates, two very wise men, but two very different destinies. Great wisdom is no guarantee of anything. But to those who really care about it, wisdom is its own reward. Socrates could have avoided prosecution as a criminal if he would have just admitted that he was wrong.

KNOW WHO YOU ARE

You could make a case that agreeing to be executed when you could avoid it by just saying a few words is not very wise. Perhaps, not even smart. And you would be right if it were you or me in that position. But it was the right thing to do for Socrates because he really knew who he was. And he knew that what gave his life meaning and made it worth living was his manner of asking questions and trying to answer them honestly.

After all, what would the rest of your life be like if you were to suddenly become dishonest to yourself after dedicating yourself so long to honesty and wisdom? Socrates knew who he was and what his life meant. And he understood that even one bit of lip service in his last moments would undo all of the good and meaningful questions he had been asking for more than seventy years.

"Is that wisdom?" you may ask once again. And again, I would answer with a question, like Socrates, "Wisdom for whom? For you and me? Or for the wisest man in Greece?"

What might be wise for you and me who possibly could live quite happily despite knowing that we had compromised our beliefs, would not be wise for someone who had totally dedicated himself to seeking the truth. "Know thyself," was Socrates' motto. He knew himself well enough to realize that he had to drink that cup of poison and his character was strong enough so that he was actually able to do it.

STAYING ON IN LIFE

I know a few people who make their living as personal financial planners. They help individuals and families define their individual needs today and in the coming years. And they help people do what must be done to provide for those needs. Any good personal financial planner will tell you that most people are insufficiently prepared for retirement. And I would add that this lack of preparedness is not limited to the financial sphere. For a mature human being, there has to be some higher value or truth than just staying on in life. Just catching a few more gasps of air. Or even having a large enough retirement income so that you can spend your final years on the golf course.

In my work, I talk a lot about what conclusions you should draw if you are not wealthy by the time you are fifty or sixty years of age. How it is an indication of poor planning or poor self-management. If you are fifty or sixty and haven't really thought about what more there is or who you are and why you're here and what your life means, well, you just haven't provided for your old age. Don't worry about a financial planner, you need a personal wisdom consultant.

Part of wisdom is knowing what you lack, looking for it, and asking for it. Another part of wisdom is knowing, at the same time as you ask, that there are no final answers. There are always more questions. There are always more things and people you don't now know, haven't heard of or seen.

You may have a retirement package, medical benefits, pension, a sunbelt home, and a steady income you can live on, but what good is it if you are isolated? And I don't mean just physically alone. I mean isolated from a real sense of connection with what has come before and with what lies ahead. This is when wisdom provides very real, very practical benefits. Wisdom provides a sense of life's value and assurance that all of life's efforts have been worthwhile.

There is no question that we must take care of our material needs. But a fulfilled life requires meaning as well as substance. Wisdom is the truth of experience. Experience is something everyone acquires if they live long enough. But not everyone knows what to do with it. Wisdom comes from seeing the world and the people in it—and from noticing patterns and connections and using what other people let you see of themselves to understand your own self.

I can hear somebody thinking, *Wait a minute, you spent a lot of paragraphs writing that nobody knows what wisdom is. Now you are giving a detailed description of it.* Well, I'm not saying I know what wisdom is. I'm just saying I know where it comes from. I know what it takes to get it. In fact, I've never met a person who actually said, "I know what wisdom is."

About as close as I'll ever come to saying that is to say, "I know what the opposite of a wise person is." The opposite of a wise person is a fool. And a fool usually gets treated like a fool sooner or later.

THE ESSENTIAL ONENESS

There is a story about a man who spent his whole life traveling to the far corners of the earth to seek out some sage, master, or yogi, who would tell him the meaning of life. The seeker crosses the deserts and oceans. He starves and suffers. And finally he is on his last legs with his rags blowing off his back in tatters. As he crawls to the mouth of a cave where an old man wearing nothing but a hair shirt and a long gray beard is sitting cross-legged in the snow. "What is the meaning of life?" gasps the seeker of truth.

The old yogi suddenly looks very surprised. "What!" he exclaims. "The meaning of life is 'What'?"

I knew a wise man once, a man I had really come to admire. I wanted very badly to define the essence of his wisdom; to isolate exactly what was the source of his great insight into life. So I finally asked him, "What is it that really makes you different from everyone else?"

And he said, "What makes me different is that I can see we are all the same. Anybody can see the differences between people. Wisdom is understanding how we are really alike."

Abraham Lincoln used to say things like that. And in my opinion, he is one of the most admirable individuals in all of history. Lincoln was a man with a very strong sense of right and wrong. He led this country through the Civil War because he knew that it was just plain wrong for one man to own another as a slave. But he also understood that the man on the other side of the issue, the person across the battle line, was a human being, too. With the same hopes, fears, and problems as the people on Lincoln's side. Despite all of the differences, Lincoln saw the essential sameness, the essential oneness.

Like Lincoln, Albert Einstein came from humble beginnings. Not just financially, but the way he was looked upon by other people. When he was a young boy, Einstein was thought to be stupid. He even flunked elementary mathematics. He was always a little distracted, asking questions but not able to put the questions into words. Even when he grew up and worked in the Swiss patent office, nobody guessed that Einstein was still asking questions that would shake the whole world.

After he published his book *Theory of Relativity,* which laid the foundation of the atomic age, Einstein didn't get a swelled head. He kept asking questions about who we are, why we are here, and why the universe was made. Even after he found answers to some of the most profound scientific questions that had ever been put forward, Einstein remained an essentially humble person. He never suggested that his answers were the final ones. Why should they be? After all, everything in the universe is subject to change. With the single exception being the speed of light—and Einstein had made that discovery himself.

People of wisdom are much more interested in questions than in answers. But foolish people are always coming back to conclusions. Like success, wisdom is a process, not a destination.

Am I a wise person? I've been talking so much about wisdom, you must be wondering about my qualifications. I suppose everyone who manages to survive and even prosper to some extent has moments of self-satisfaction. Moments when you say to yourself, *I finally have it all figured out once and for all.* But usually something comes along, pretty quickly, to humble you.

I was sitting on an airplane traveling from Texas to California and looking out the windows at the mountains and

Like success, wisdom is a process, not a destination.

the desert far below. I was thinking to myself how until quite recently in the span of human history, nobody had ever seen anything like this, none of the kings and queens, none of the warriors, none of the wizards. Nobody had ever been able to fly forty thousand feet in the air and look down on the mountains. How powerful we have suddenly come. Today all we have to do is buy an airline ticket and we can do something that no one back then even dreamed would be possible.

For a moment or two, all of this gave me a feeling of power. It felt pretty good looking down on everything. But then I thought, *Wait a minute, can I stop the plane or turn it around? Can I take a walk outside and then come back to my seat? I can't even take a walk around the plane unless the little light tells me it's okay. I can't even feed myself in here. In all of my adult life, I've never been less powerful than I am at this very moment. I'm completely helpless.*

It is that way with wisdom, too. When you think you really know something, stop for a second and see if the opposite isn't really true as well. Do you think you are it? Compared to whom? Maybe you are really poor. Do you think you are poor? Compared to whom? Maybe you are really rich....

WHO'S THE WISER

Picture a crowded subway car in New York City. Quite an experience, but not something I would recommend to the faint of heart. Hundreds of complete strangers jammed into a space designed for a third the number. All of them packed tighter than sardines in a little tiny can. Now you are in that situation and you have been on your feet all day and you would really like to sit down. But there are no seats left in the subway car; so you are standing there hanging from the metal bar that hangs from the ceiling.

Do you suppose you could come up with something that would convince somebody to give you their seat? That's a pretty good test of wisdom, in my opinion. You'd have to be pretty wise to come up with something like that in a crowded New York subway car. Frankly, I don't think King Solomon could have done it. I don't think Socrates could have done it. I don't even believe Einstein could have done it.

But then it happened. Somebody convinces not just one person, but several people to offer their seats. People are actually competing to give up their precious seats in that crowded New York subway car. Who is this somebody? A pregnant woman, a very pregnant woman, in fact. But it wasn't really the woman who convinced them to do it. It was the baby inside. It was a tiny person who couldn't talk, or even imagine the very idea of talking, who convinced these New Yorkers to stand up.

Einstein couldn't have done that, "Excuse me, my name is Albert Einstein, perhaps you have heard of me? Do you think I could have your seat here in the subway?"

"Never heard of you, Einstein, get lost."

"But I am very wise."

"Yeah, well, you are wising off to the wrong guy."

So am I saying an unborn baby is wiser than Albert Einstein? Maybe you should decide. But that baby certainly solved the problem.

ASK DIFFERENT QUESTIONS

Here is a phrase that I am pretty sure contains some important wisdom: "If you have reached the point in life where you feel you have all the answers, you better start asking some different questions." The fool is always reaching his intellectual destination. The wise man is always wondering how much further there is to go.

The fool's viewpoint is always narrowing. These people talk more and more but they listen less and less all the time. They say the same thing repeatedly because they are always thinking the same thoughts. If they are powerful fools, people are eager to help them along. Particularly if they're dependent upon them for their living. But people are laughing at the fools behind their back—and are watching and waiting for the moment when they become vulnerable.

As an illustration, a big-league baseball game scene. A pitcher gets into an argument with the umpire. The pitcher has been covering first base on the bunt. But the ump calls the runner safe. So the pitcher just stands there with the ball in his hand, yelling and arguing, because he is sure he is right. He is sure the runner should be called out. But of course the whole time he is arguing, the runner keeps running. The pitcher is so sure he is right; he is so totally wrapped up in his own wisdom, that the runner runs all the way around the bases and scores.

You've probably seen things like that happen. A person who is so convinced of their own wisdom that they cause more damage than any fool. It doesn't only happen on the baseball diamond. Stay away from people like that. And if you find yourself behaving like that, get a different baseball glove, because it is high time you stopped pitching and started catching for a while.

My father once told me, "I've seen a lot of wicked people and a lot of foolish ones, and I believe they both get what they deserve in the end. But the foolish ones get it first." I've found that to be true. In a way, it is the opposite of the idea and the saying that "Ignorance is bliss." In fact, ignorance is *not* bliss, it's misery, it's poverty of the mind and spirit—and sooner or later poverty of the bank account as well.

Wisdom is the wealth of the heart, mind, and soul. And unlike money, once you have it, no one and nothing can ever take it away from you. Once you have come to possess it, wisdom is yours forever. And even when you pass it on to others, your own store of it grows.

5

RESPONSIBILITY

Most people dread accepting responsibility. That's just a fact of life. And we can see it in operation every day. We get hot under the collar when the dentist keeps us waiting and we are sitting there reading old magazines when our appointment was thirty minutes ago. And we don't stop to think that we forgot to mail in this month's mortgage payment.

We grow angrier and angrier because a business contact is supposed to call at noon, and it's at almost two o'clock and the phone still refuses to ring. But we don't stop to think about the calls we forgot to return while so busy fuming. We can see ourselves writing an angry letter to the airlines because a flight was delayed. But we don't write an angry letter to ourselves when we are late for a meeting, even though that might not be a bad idea at all.

Yes, we can see avoidance of responsibility all the time, in both our personal and professional lives.

And here is something else we can see just as often, people aren't as successful as they wish they were. There is a connection between these two very common phenomena, and by the end of this chapter, I hope you will agree with me. I hope you will understand that it is in your best interest to take responsibility for everything you do—but that's only the beginning. I'm also going to suggest that many times it's even best to accept responsibility for the mistakes of others—especially when you are in a managerial or leadership role.

I can almost hear you saying, "What? Accept responsibility for someone else's mess up? Why would I want to do something like that?" Well, that's a fair enough question, and over the next few pages, I'll try to answer.

During the years when professional basketball was just beginning to become really popular, Bill Russell, who played center for the Boston Celtics, was one of the greatest players in the pro league. He was especially known for his rebounding and defensive skills. But like a lot of very tall centers, Russell was never much of a free throw shooter. His free throw percentage was quite a bit below average, in fact. But this low percentage didn't really give a clear picture of Russell as an athlete—and in one game he gave a very convincing demonstration of this.

It was the final game of a championship series between Boston and the Los Angeles Lakers. With about twelve seconds left to play, the Lakers were behind by one point. And Boston had the ball. It was obvious that the Lakers would have to foul one of Boston's players to get the ball back. And they chose to foul Bill Russell. This was a perfectly logical choice since statistically, Russell was the worst free throw shooter on the court at that moment. If he missed the shot, the Lakers would probably get the ball back and they would still have enough time to try to win the game. But if Russell made his first free throw, the Lakers' chances would be seriously diminished. And if he made both shots, the game would essentially be over.

Bill Russell had a very peculiar style of shooting free throws. Today, no self-respecting basketball player anywhere in America would attempt it. Aside from the question of whether it is an effective way to shoot a basket, it just looked too ridiculous. Whenever he had to shoot a free throw, the six-foot-eleven Russell would start off holding the ball in both hands about waist high. Then he'd squat down, and as he straightened up he would let go of the ball. It looked like he was trying to throw a bucket of dirt over a wall.

But regardless of how he looked, as soon as Bill Russell was fouled he knew the Celtics were going to win the game. He was absolutely certain of it. Because in a situation like this, statistics and percentages mean nothing. There was a much more important factor at work. Something that no one has found a way to express in numbers and decimal points. Simply put, Bill Russell was the player who wanted to take responsibility for the success or failure of his team.

He wanted the weight on his shoulders in a situation like this. No possibility for excuses, no possibility of blaming anyone else if the game was lost, no second-guessing. Bill Russell wanted the ball in his own hands and nobody else's. And like magic, even if he had missed every free throw he had missed in his life before this, he knew he was going to make this one. And that is exactly what happened.

That happens when a man or woman accepts responsibility eagerly and with confidence. I have always felt that accepting responsibility is one of the highest forms of human maturity. A willingness to be accountable. To put yourself on the line is really the defining characteristic of adulthood.

Anyone who has raised children knows how true this is. Just look at a baby during the first few years of life. Every

Putting yourself on the line is the defining characteristic of adulthood.

gesture, every facial expression, every tentative word has one message for the baby's parents: "I am totally dependent on you. I can't do anything for myself even if I try. I can't be held responsible for the consequences; after all, I'm just a baby."

Ten or twelve years later, of course, as the boy or girl enters adolescence, this message to the parents will be very different. It will sound something like, "Why don't you just leave me alone; I want to be totally independent. I don't want to do anything but think about myself. I certainly don't want to accept any responsibility for anything beyond my own very well-defined needs and desires."

It's only when we at last grow up that the first two messages; "I am totally dependent on you" and "I am totally independent of you," finally turn into, "You can depend on me." Which is the truly adult outlook.

Strange as it may seem, of course, there are people in their thirties and forties who are still acting like adolescents. And there are even people in their forties and fifties who are still acting like babies, as far as their attitude toward responsibility is concerned. These kinds of people can be hard to have around, especially if you have to work with them.

But interestingly, a large number of people who shirk responsibility can also provide opportunities for you. If you are determined to be different and decide to be one of the few who embraces responsibility, you can lead, and you will deserve to lead.

Winston Churchill said, "The price of greatness is responsibility." And in my opinion, it is really rather a small price to pay. Let me be more specific about exactly what is involved in becoming a responsible person. It means first of all that you accept the consequences of your actions—but I will go even further than that. Responsibility means you look to yourself as a source of everything that happens to you. It means that you assume command, regardless of the hardships you may have undergone early in life or the prejudice you may have encountered, or the dozens of people who may have failed to understand you.

Do you detect a note of irony in those statements, or perhaps a note of sarcasm? Do I sound hard-hearted? Do I seem to be denying the existence of difficult childhoods, prejudice, or of people who are insensitive to the needs of others? Well that is certainly not my intention or my belief.

I'm saying that regardless of the presence of negative influences in your life, the best thing you can do, the most empowering thing, the strongest thing, and ultimately the wisest thing is to accept responsibility for your own destiny, plain and simple.

ACCEPT RESPONSIBILITY FOR YOUR DESTINY

The benefits of this approach to life have been proven in some pretty dramatic ways. People who have been afflicted by serious illness, for example, appear to have a better chance of recovery if they decide to take responsibility for what has happened to them. Despite the fact that it would be easier, and perhaps even more reasonable to simply see themselves as victims of fate.

There is a man, let's call him John, who had been healthy and vigorous all of his life. He had started and sold businesses in a number of different fields before finally deciding to enter school in his late forties. At that time, however, he began to suffer some severe health problems. All of his life, his main focus had been on success and achievement. He really hadn't paid much attention to what was happening to his body.

For years, John subsisted largely on a diet of donuts and black coffee. And because he traveled a great deal, he also consumed large amounts of airplane food. Inexorably, he was gaining weight, five pounds one year, ten pounds the next year, fifteen pounds the year after that. Of course, John responded by opening a number of stores that featured clothing for overweight men. And he even used himself in his advertising. In retrospect, this was probably a mistake. It gave him an incentive to gain even more weight. One year John gained twenty pounds and actually bragged about that fact in his newspaper ad.

Then he was diagnosed with severe diabetes. Although John's physicians assured him that the disease was brought about as much by heredity as by behavioral patterns, he was the kind of man who believed that he was the captain of his own ship—not a common sailor taking orders from someone higher up. He was a man of strong character. And now in the face of this new challenge, John resolved to take responsibility for his own well-being.

As he explained it, "All my adult life I have been preoccupied with supporting my family and getting ahead financially. It was a sense of responsibility that I felt. And to a large extent, I've lived up to it. But I can see now that responsibility is beginning to express itself in a different way. Providing for my family is not just a matter of dollars and cents anymore. It's a matter of staying alive; it's my health and the health of my family that's at stake as well."

John continued, "I'm not setting a good example for my kids. They have seen me gaining weight; they've seen me literally brag about it in my advertisements. And lately, they have been gaining weight themselves. I think in some sense they believe this is what I want them to do. And maybe they are not completely wrong. In fact, I've been thinking of including my kids in some new advertising; and depending on how it goes over, I've had it in my mind to open up some clothing stores for overweight youngsters.

John's eyes began to light up at the thought of expanding his business and expanding new opportunities. But then he caught himself. And as he continued to speak he pounded his fist on the table. "There I go again," he said. "I've got myself locked into a certain kind of thinking. And now I have to get myself out of it. It is as simple as that."

It was clear that John was into a few well-defined thought patterns. But the most important one was the way he saw himself as the cause of everything that happened. Not only in his own life, but in the lives of others.

The doctors told him his diabetes might have come on even if he hadn't been overeating and overworking. But John knew that was nonsense. And as far as his kids were concerned, there have been a lot of news reports documenting the fact that American kids, in general, are heavier than they used to be. They just don't get the same amount of exercise as the kids of previous generations.

John could have resigned himself that his kids, like just about all kids today, are going to watch television, play video games, and eat junk food, whether he gained weight or not. But he didn't. "Bologna," he said, "It is all my fault and I'm going to do something about it. In fact, I'm going to do a *lot* about it." And he did do a lot about it.

John radically changed his diet and his lifestyle. He began ordering vegetarian meals on plane flights. He became a fitness enthusiast and ran several marathons. Although he ran rather slowly as you might expect of a man in his fifties, he took pride in the fact that he always ran the course three times, on the day before the race, on the official race day, and again on the day after.

Instead of opening a clothing store for overweight children and using his own kids in the advertisements, he consulted a behavioral psychologist who helped him devise a system of financial rewards for his children that helped them bring their weight down. A system that taught them something about money at the same time.

John is now in significantly better physical shape, is entering his final year of law school, and is negotiating with several companies to market his behavioral science techniques for reversing juvenile obesity.

Sooner or later, all of us face situations in which we must decide whether to *accept* responsibility for a problem or look for ways to *avoid* responsibility. Assuming that you have in fact, done something that has caused a problem of some kind.

INTENTION

Let's look at the various options and decisions that are open to you. First, there is the role played by *intention*. In other words, was the outcome of your action what you intended it to be? And if it was not, should you still accept responsibility for that outcome? This is a very serious issue in the way we think about responsibility in our society.

In many areas of criminal law, for instance, the intention to commit a crime must be present in order for the accused to be held criminally responsible. This intention is something quite different from mere negligence. If you leave your garden hose lying across the sidewalk so that the mailman trips over it and breaks his leg, you may be held responsible in a civil suit. But you would not be prosecuted as a criminal in the way you would be, for instance, if you had used a weapon in a robbery or an assault.

But we don't have to enter a courtroom to see the important role intention plays in accepting responsibility ourselves or assigning it to others. Do you remember when you were a kid and you left the screen door open and the family pet ran outside and was lost all afternoon? What did you say to avoid responsibility? You said, "I didn't mean to do that." You said, "It was an accident." As pointed out earlier, there are a lot of people who still use these child-like rationalizations well into their middle age.

But if and when you decide you want to be an adult, you begin to see the whole question of intention as nothing more than another opportunity for excuse-making. And you should refuse to participate in it. The great thing about excuses, and the really dangerous thing about them, is that no matter what happens, excuses are always there waiting to be used. Anybody can have an excuse for absolutely anything. And people have never been better at it than they are today.

But the downside of excuses, even good ones, is that nobody really believes them. I don't care what people tell you, if you make excuses, they are going to know it and they are going to think less of you. But if you refuse to rely on excuses, people are going to know that too—and they will admire you for it.

This is especially true in business. One of the classic examples happened about fifteen years ago. A widely advertised product from a leading manufacturer was shown to be unsafe. And the company responded by pulling every box off of the shelves at a cost of millions of dollars. Was the company destroyed? Hardly. If they had done anything else, there would have been a tremendous loss of confidence. Both on the part of consumers and employees. Instead, there was honest acceptance of responsibility for a mistake. And the public image of the company was dramatically enhanced.

Contrast this with what happened recently with a leading manufacturer of computer chips. When a new microprocessor didn't perform up to expectations, the company made excuses. It was a minor problem, something that would crop up once in a lifetime, and so forth. Were these excuses valid? Maybe, maybe not. But it doesn't really matter, does it?

So many people use excuses, but nobody really believes them. It's our modern version fable about the *Boy Who Called Wolf.* In this case, the computer chip manufacturer finally took so much heat that they did replace the processor, which is what they should have done in the first place.

NOT MYSELF AT THE TIME

An off-shoot of the, "I didn't mean to do it" excuse for evading responsibility, is the "I wasn't myself at the time" excuse. This really deserves to be a category all its own. Particularly since it has received so much attention in the courts, where it often occurs in the form of a defense based on temporary insanity, or some other stress-related syndrome.

A friend tells me about one day when she flew from Texas to Los Angeles for a joint presentation she would be making along with a fellow from New York City. They had planned it all out very carefully over the phone. A lot of documents had been assembled. But they both knew that what really counts in face-to-face meetings is personal impressions.

On this score, my friend felt very confident about the LA meeting, because her guy from New York City was an extremely charismatic personality. A burly and bearded man, always ready with a joke. He never wore a business suit, his trademark outfit was a plaid shirt worn with the sleeves rolled up, a loosely knotted knit tie, khaki slacks, and loafers.

His favorite expression was, "Let's get the show on the road." And he always said it with such gusto that he sounded like a nineteenth-century wagon master starting a wagon train up the Oregon Trail. Most of all, he could sell refrigerators to the Eskimos. And of course, she was confident because he was always so good at selling himself.

You can imagine my friend's extreme surprise and deep disappointment when this usually energetic ball of fire completely dropped the ball in their presentation. When they met in their client's outer office, my friend could hardly believe what she was seeing. The guy from New York was just sitting there, almost like a lump. He had no energy whatsoever, like every bit of vitality had been drained out of him. When the meeting actually got underway, he seemed to grow even more lethargic, while my friend was left trying to pick up the slack. She was puzzled and could see the incomprehension on the faces of the people she'd traveled all this way to meet.

Here was this big guy in a plaid shirt, all but slumped over like the mouse at Alice in Wonderland's Tea Party. Was anybody going to invest money in that man's ideas? He seemed about as dynamic as a sack of potatoes. As you might expect, it wasn't long before they were safely outside the building, and my friend wasted no time in asking what in the world was wrong?

In response, this usually energetic man in his lumberjack shirt said something about jet lag. "It was all because of jet lag," he explained. He just wasn't himself. The flight from New York had been just too much. He'd feel better in a day or so, but for the time being, he was just not the man he normally was. He just wasn't himself.

Well, it was all she could do to keep from laughing in his face. Here was a guy who looked like a wagon master leading settlers across the continent, and he was put totally out of commission by a first-class flight from New York City. What could she say? "Jet lag? Is that the problem?" she asked. "Is that all?"

"Well, not exactly," he replied. "There is something else." Now she grew more concerned. Obviously something was deeply worrying this man. It could be anything. Maybe he had been diagnosed with a serious illness, or perhaps someone in his family was ill. Maybe his house had burned down. Maybe he was in serious financial trouble.

"It's okay," she said, trying to sound calm for her own bene-fit as well as for her colleague. "Do you want to talk about it?"

He nodded, "It's sad."

"Well, I'm sure it is. But I'm also sure you'll be able to handle it."

For the first time all day, he smiled a weak little smile. "No," he said, "you don't understand. SAD is an acronym for Seasonal Affective Disorder." As my friend listened with amazement, he went on to explain that his jet lag had been worsened by the effects of Seasonal Affective Disorder. A mood disorder brought on by the short chilly days of winter. "You are out here in the West where it doesn't really get all that cold." He concluded, sounding totally miserable. "You don't really know what it is like."

Of course my friend knew what it's like. We all know what it's like, it's excuses, evasion of responsibility. Acting like a child. Refusing to grow up. You can call it jet lag, or SAD, or whatever you want—it doesn't really matter what you call it. My friend wanted to tell him what she really thought of his psycho-babble, but she knew what the "class" move really was here. And she wanted to make the class move because she wanted to exhibit a strong character. And remember, a strong character assumes responsibility. If you want to be a leader in any walk of life, you must choose to assume responsibility for whatever happens, whether you have to or not.

It's like being at the helm of a ship. You are responsible for everything that takes place on your watch. "Don't worry about it," she said. "I should have been ready to carry the meeting by myself. Next time I'll be better prepared." Then she caught a cab back to the airport.

Let me elaborate a little bit further on the relationship between responsibility and leadership. Bear Bryant once said something about this issue. Bryant was the coach of many great football teams at the University of Alabama. And until his record was broken recently, he had the highest number of victories of any coach in the history of the game. Bryant said that from his point of view, it was impossible for any of his players to make a mistake during a football game. Any and all mistakes were his because as a coach he was solely and completely responsible for preparing his athletes to play error-free football.

By saying this, Bryant was truly accepting a leadership role and he was embracing the special category of responsibility that comes with it. As a leader, you have to own responsibility for preparing subordinates for the challenges they'll face. And if the result is not successful, you have to accept responsibility for not having prepared them adequately. Maybe this seems like a harsh standard to live up to, but that's just the way it is. If you can't handle responsibility and leadership, at least admit it to yourself and don't let other people start depending

Choose the standard you want to live by and follow through.

on you. Choose the standard you want to live by and follow through on it.

In the ancient world, during the time of the Roman Empire, there was an interesting attitude toward this kind of choice-making. It was a brutal world in those days, to say the least. Anything could happen, from plagues to revolutions, to barbarian invasions. Even for the upper classes, it was a challenge just to survive. Yet, certain people attempted to do more. There was a tradition whereby people attempted to create themselves, and their characters, exactly the way an artist would create a painting or a sculpture.

Like a work of art, these people looked upon their lives and their characters as things of beauty that would live on after their deaths in the memories of their friends and families. People who chose to live their lives this way were not monks, aesthetics, or in any way removed from life and the every-day world. They were just very serious about building strong character.

Roman emperor Marcus Aurelius is a famous example of this type of person. His journal is a powerful example of every-thing involved in building character and leadership. Much of it was written in military camps while the emperor was leading the Roman armies against barbarian tribes in what is now Germany. The writings of this ancient emperor and of other people from the same period reflect a conscious choice to live according to certain standards of responsibility and character.

This kind of clear decision about how to build your inner self is something that we rarely see today. Most people want to be good. They want to be ethical, moral, and successful in

"I slept and dreamed that life was beauty. I woke and saw that life was duty."

every way. They want to fulfill their potential. But they think it's something that will just happen itself. They don't see that there should be a conscious, ongoing acceptance of responsibility for what you do and who you really are.

There is a saying that goes, "I slept and dreamed that life was beauty. I woke and saw that life was duty." If you want to be really in control of your life and if you want other people to be able to depend on you and look to you for leadership, you must wake up from the dream that somebody else will handle the pressure. That somebody else will shoot those two free throws.

Accepting responsibility doesn't mean that life can't be beautiful. But it does mean opening your eyes to the realities. A successful person must not only accept but eagerly desire to accept responsibility. It means making a conscious decision to grow up, to let go of the dependency needs of childhood and adolescence, and recreate yourself as someone other people can depend on. It means wanting the ball when the game is on the line.

6

HUMOR, CHARACTER, LEADERSHIP

A duck walked into a large discount store and went up and down the aisles filling his shopping cart with goods. He then pushed the cart up to the check-out area. The clerk took a look at the full shopping cart and was a little surprised by the large amount of stuff the duck had gathered. "Will that be cash or charge?" the clerk politely asked. The duck looked at him a little impatiently and said, "Hey, I'm in kind of a hurry, just put it all on my bill."

That was a joke you've probably heard before. As this chapter is about humor and its role in character and leadership, I thought it would be a good idea to start off with a joke. In fact, it's almost always a good idea to let people know you have a good sense of humor. In today's society, we take humor very seriously. And by the way, you have a good sense of humor, don't you? I'm confident you'll answer in the affirmative. Because virtually everyone is sure they have a good sense of humor. We discuss that comment later.

Right now, though, I want to emphasize how important humor is as an aspect of strong character. Yet, if you were to ask a hundred people to name character's most vital elements, I doubt if more than five would refer to humor. In fact, I don't think any would.

When he wrote his classic study of American society in the early eighteenth century, the Frenchman Alexis de Tocqueville predicted that if the United States ever came to be ruled by a dictator, it would be someone with a well-developed sense of humor. If this is true, it's certainly a very different situation than you would find in any other country in the world. Think of the communist and fascist dictators who played such major roles in twentieth-century history. They were not exactly a bunch of laugh-a-minute guys. Rather, they were good at projecting anger and creating fear. But humor? No.

Americans, however, respond to very different qualities in their leaders. And though they were obviously not dictators or tyrants, it's true that most of our beloved national leaders have had the ability to make others laugh and to laugh at themselves. Though he was fundamentally a rather melancholy man, Abraham Lincoln was also renowned as a humorist. Every biography of Lincoln refers to his love of funny stories. And his willingness to stop and tell a joke even in the midst of important business.

In more recent times, President Franklin Roosevelt, John Kennedy, and Ronald Reagan were able to smooth out the ups and downs of their political careers with humor. And it was often directed at themselves. People could see that these men were strong enough and confident enough to make jokes at their own expense. And, as we will discuss later, these men were also wise enough to apply humor carefully and at the right time.

When we recognize those abilities in a person, we believe they'll also be strong and confident in serious or even dangerous situations. In short, Americans see a well-developed sense of humor as an aspect of a strong character—almost a prerequisite for leadership.

But before you go out and buy a joke book as part of your personal self-development program, here's the bad news. To a great extent, you can't learn to be humorous. And that alone makes humor different from every other trait we've discussed so far in this book.

There are many examples of people who learn to overcome fear, or even downright cowardice, who went on to become courageous leaders. There are fools who learned to be wise. And there are liars who turned into honest men and women. There are rigid thinkers who learned flexibility. But I personally have never encountered a humorless person who learned to be humorous. And if there were such a person, I'm sure I would have come across one by now, because I have certainly encountered a great many humorless people.

HUMOR AND HONESTY

Perhaps one reason we respond so strongly to humor in our leaders is because we associate it with honesty. I think this association is well-founded. Real humor is honest because real humor can't be faked. You can pretend to be serious, just like you can pretend to be intelligent—we can always fake those qualities, and some people do it all the time. But you can't really pretend to be funny.

The real irony, however, is that nobody feels like they have to fake having a good sense of humor. Because everybody thinks that they actually have one. People will admit to almost anything before they confess to being humorless. Have you ever met anyone who said, "You know, I just don't know how to laugh. I just don't like it when things are funny. I'm just more comfortable being serious all the time." I've never met anyone like that, and I am very confident that I never will. In fact, if somebody actually confessed to me that he didn't have any sense of humor, I would think he must be joking.

Take, for example, a fellow named Sam. Sam was about as dour an individual as you would ever want to meet. He was in the meatpacking industry, which isn't an especially amusing occupation, to begin with. In his spare time he was always trying to discover ways to make a quick million dollars. He had really been influenced by the hula-hoop fad that swept the country during the summer of 1958. For some reason, that summer all the kids in America decided they had to have a hula-hoop. Consequently, the company that manufactured them made a huge amount of money. Sam was captivated by this phenomenon. It really fired his imagination.

Although he made very good money with his meatpacking business. He was determined to recreate the hula-hoop. He spent thousands of dollars trying to develop or find new toys. Some of them were very clever but there was one contraption that involved a block of wood on a string. I'm not sure how it was supposed to work, but if a kid wasn't careful and swung it around a little too fast, anybody standing nearby would be knocked cold. In any case, there was something very funny about seeing this totally humorless man, Sam, who was already quite wealthy, trying to make millions with silly toys.

After a while, there was also something a little sad about it. Because there really was only one hula-hoop fad, Sam was clearly not going to recreate it. One day a coworker of Sam's finally decided to have a talk with him. This coworker was quite a bit younger, so he approached Sam very deferentially, saying, "Sam, I'm a little confused. You're interested in making money on a new toy. But you're actually losing a lot of money trying to develop them or importing them from South America. Tell me a little bit about what you think is going on here."

Sam just looked at him and sighed. He said, "This business we are in is a pretty grim way of making money. I have to have something going on the side. I have to have something to keep my mind off making sausage and hamburger."

To which the coworker replied, "Sam, I can certainly understand that. And I sympathize with how you feel. But you just don't seem to have a real knack for the toy business. Why don't you get involved with something that you are good at? Something that would let you use your natural abilities."

Sam was silent for a moment, thinking it over. When he concentrated like that his chin sank down against his chest and he looked like an old hound dog. He really seemed to have the weight of the entire world on his shoulders. He looked like he had just lost his best friend in the world.

Finally he looked up and said, "Well, I've always had an excellent sense of humor, maybe I could do something with that." Since that conversation, Sam has been trying his hand at writing scripts for television comedy. Wouldn't it be interesting, and disturbing, if one of them were set in a slaughterhouse?

A man or a woman will admit to anything before they admit to being a sourpuss. It just doesn't happen. But it's not like they secretly know they're humorless and they're trying to keep it to themselves. It's not like they secretly know they have this great weakness, which is not having a sense of humor. That's not the way it is at all. No, every gloomy-gus really thinks he is a very funny guy.

Sam, the meatpacker was a perfect example of that. Like everybody else, he thought he had a very good sense of humor. And he even thought he might be able to cash in on it somehow. That's one of the reasons that humor is such a mysterious and elusive quality.

A MYSTERIOUS AND ELUSIVE QUALITY

No doubt you've seen gangster movies where the head of the mob makes some terrible joke and all of the guys sitting around the table have to keep laughing until he lets them know it's safe to stop. That doesn't just happen among gangsters; that happens every day in the corporate boardroom and congressional offices. It even happens around family dinner tables.

Since everybody deeply believes that they have a good sense of humor, how can you find out if you actually don't? Unfortunately, you probably can't. It's just a very tough situation to deal with. Even your best friends won't tell you that you're a humorless wet blanket. Fortunately, I'm not. I wake up every day feeling thankful for my good sense of humor; and in that sense, I'm sure I'm just like everybody else.

I wrote that the lack of humor has characterized dictators throughout history. That's true because real humor is almost always subversive. Humor undermines dictatorial power. It punctures balloons. It knocks people off pedestals. Nothing enraged Adolf Hitler more than Charlie Chaplin's portrayal of him in the movie called, *The Great Dictator*. Chaplin, who was actually born on the same day as Hitler, did a fantastic job of capturing the dictator's every nuance and mannerism. This movie did more to alert the American people to the real nature of the Nazi dictatorship than any book or news report available at the time.

Powerful people and the symbols of power that they like to accumulate are rarely humorous, at least intentionally. Think of the Russian generals with all those rows of ribbons on their uniforms. Whatever else you may want to say about them, it was obvious that those uniforms were supposed to be very serious. A dozen rows of ribbons, a big red star on the hat, all sorts of gold braid hanging everywhere—hey, this is no laughing matter.

What a wonderful irony then, that humor played an important part in the downfall of the Soviet Union. In the final years of the communist regime, political jokes became a highly developed art form in Russia and all of the countries of Eastern Europe. And the generals didn't get the joke until it was too late.

CATEGORIES OF LAUGHTER

The anti-government jokes that were circulating in the Soviet Union during its final years were an example of a particular kind of humor. They were designed to elicit a very specific kind of response, which we can call the *Laughter of Ridicule*. This is really a form of hostility disguised as mirth. It's intended to be very destructive to its target; and at the same time, it serves as a kind of a survival mechanism for the joke-teller and the listeners. It allows them to express their anger indirectly.

If you are ever in a leadership position and you find that this kind of hostile humor has been directed at you, I strongly suggest that you do one thing immediately—ask yourself what you have been doing to provoke this kind of response among your subordinates. When you figure it out, I suggest you change that behavior immediately. Laughter of ridicule is a very bad sign for a leader. It's one kind of humor that should be taken very seriously.

There are several other categories of laughter that we should consider as well. Have you ever gone to a comedy movie and noticed that the audience starts laughing even before anything funny happens? A leading comic actor can simply come on the screen, and make a bland remark about the weather, and everyone in the audience will start laughing. I've seen this happen many times with people like Robin Williams and Steve Martin. Underlying this kind of laughter is a desire on the part of people to have a shared experience; they want to participate in the experience together. I call this the *Laughter of Community*.

Another kind of laughter that can be observed at the movies is something I call the *Laughter of Recognition*. This occurs when people want to show that they get the joke. They see how something was intended to be funny, even if less-informed people don't see it. This kind of laughter is common, especially among younger audiences. And many members of the older generation find themselves frequently missing out on it.

Irony is the basis for so much humor today. And by its very nature, irony is intended to exclude a certain percentage of people. The rest of them laugh to show that they have been admitted to the club. They laugh to show they recognize the joke; and therefore, deserve to be recognized as members of that select group. That's why I call it the *Laughter of Recognition.*

Polite Laughter is yet another category that one gets when a laughing response is called for but isn't really motivated. We've all had the experience of telling a joke that doesn't really go over too well and elicits only polite laughter. And we've all responded to such jokes with polite laughter of our own. It's just a gesture that keeps the ball rolling, but it is an important one. Nobody likes to be on the receiving end of polite laughter, "But it's better than being poked in the eye with a sharp stick," to quote an old joke.

The last and most important category of laughter I'll mention might be called, *Real Laughter,* which is spontaneous, happy, unpremeditated, and has no hidden agenda. It happens when you see or hear something that is really funny. I'm going to spend a moment talking about this category of *Real Laughter* because it is one of the most important aspects of humor. The more real laughter you can bring into your life, the better off you will be.

REAL LAUGHTER

Kids are really our best source of knowledge about real laughter. They really put their whole selves into it. We lose that to a large extent as we get older; I'm not sure that loss can be completely avoided.

For example, think of someone, one of your own kids, a neighbor, niece, or nephew that you've watched grow up. Whatever interest this person pursues today, it's likely that he or she was a budding artist in the early years. Crayons, markers, and pads of paper are standard issue in most households with young kids. Kids draw big beautiful pictures with all sorts of colors and patterns. At that age, there are no rules about keeping inside the lines and using certain colors for certain objects. Their pictures grace refrigerators across the country and are examples of artistic genius.

Then when kids grow to about five or six years old, their drawings change. They begin drawing stick figures standing next to houses that consist of a triangle on top of a square. Kids this age are still just as proud of their drawings—and actually see them as a big advance over the ones they did as babies. They are more advanced in some ways, but they're also less free. There's a sense of responsibility about them at this age. An effort to put everything in its right place and make everything the right color and the right size.

In addition, around the same time as these kid's drawings change, their laughter changes, too. It's still delightful, but there's more awareness in it. I guess that is just the way it's got to be. As the British poet William Wordsworth put it: "Though nothing can bring back the hour of splendor in the glass and glory in the flower. We will grieve not, but rather find strength for what remains behind."

I'm sure kids have a lot of concerns and worries that seem as big to them as ours do to us. But they really don't have a lot of responsibility. They really don't have bills that have to be paid by tomorrow, or presentations or phone calls that can make your palms sweat. It's those kinds of responsibilities that suppress laughter as we get older; there is simply no avoiding it. But we should try to bring real laughter into our lives as much as we possibly can. It's good for the soul. There has even been evidence that heart-filled laughter has the ability to benefit physical health.

HUMOR IN LEADERSHIP

Let me say a few practical things about the role of humor in leadership, particularly in business or management situations. Have you ever noticed how certain jokes seem to appear in the business community, circulate for a while, and then gradually disappear? Where did these jokes come from? How do they get started? You'll hear them at the start of meetings or conferences when everybody is trying to settle down. During the course of one week, you can have meetings in Los Angeles, Phoenix, Indianapolis, and Boston, and hear the same joke in every one of those meetings. There is something almost eerie about it.

In any case, these business meeting jokes really have some important function. First, they're sort of a bonding ritual when everybody shows they share a sense of humor and that they like to laugh about the same things. I think that function is pretty obvious.

But there is another function of jokes that's more subtle but extremely important. In a way, jokes are intended to rid the situation of humor. Once the joke has been told, the humor has been encapsulated or compartmentalized within that joke, and it won't be seen again until the meeting is over. That's why it's good to begin a very serious discussion with a joke. After the moment of humor has been experienced through the joke, seriousness can reign for the balance of the meeting.

I've seen this phenomenon take place many times. If you handle it correctly, telling jokes can really reinforce your image as a serious person. Once the joke is out of the way, you can be as intense as you want for as long as you want. Because all humor has been compressed into the joke and now the joke is over and done with.

THE FUNNY GUY

There is an important distinction to be made between the leader who tells jokes and a very different kind of person I call the *funny guy*. And let me point out very quickly that the funny guy is almost always a guy. I don't believe I've ever come across a woman in business who fills this role. I'm not sure why that's true.

In any case, the funny guy doesn't seem to understand that the role of jokes is to reinforce the seriousness of the rest of the interaction. He doesn't understand that a joke is a kind of scapegoat that forms the center of a little ceremony for a moment and then is banished once and for all. No, the funny guy is someone who keeps telling jokes, who keeps reintroducing humor into a situation from which everyone else has tried to banish. I can honestly say that I've never met an effective leader whom I would identify as a funny guy. And it is even worse for the funny guy if he actually is funny. Then he is just a clown, and clowns simply are not given leadership positions in any organization.

The leaders mentioned earlier—Roosevelt, Kennedy, Reagan—used jokes and witticisms to demonstrate their humanity and to diffuse hostility. They were by no means funny guys. Often their jokes and quips weren't even funny, they were symbols of humor rather than real examples of it. And even this largely symbolic version of humor was applied very carefully. If it had been otherwise, these men would never have achieved a leadership role of any kind, let alone that of the President of the United States.

Most funny guys didn't start out that way. They're generally people who have been passed over several times and are using humor to help them cope with their disappointment. And there's also an element of anger in most funny guys. While it's usually deeply hidden and they may not even be consciously aware of it, by continuing to be funny in situations where it is no longer appropriate, the funny guy may unconsciously be trying to subvert the goals of the group. Effective leaders recognize this. They see to it that funny guys are denied any real responsibility.

Once again, and as with the other qualities we've discussed, there's something paradoxical in our attitude toward humor. We want to discover humor in other people and we want to find it in ourselves—but we don't want too much of it, and in certain situations we don't want any of it at all. Leaders intuitively understand the role of humor and they apply it in the right amounts at the right times. They understand that, as with many of the other good things in life, too much of a good thing is almost as bad as none at all.

Earlier I suggested that to a large extent humor is something that you either have or you don't. That, unlike many other self-development skills, it's very difficult to improve your capacity for humor. But if that's true, doesn't it suggest that there is something self-contradictory about this whole discussion? After all, what's the point of talking so much about humor if there is really very little you can do toward strengthening your capacity for it.

While it may be true that you can't increase the natural proportion of humor in your personality beyond a certain preordained point, that is not the end of the story. You can still learn to have a basically humorous approach to life or perhaps *playful* would be a better word. I think the ability to do so is an extremely important indicator of having a strong character.

Modern physics has demonstrated that life can act as either a particle or a wave. If we design an experiment based on light behaving like a wave, we will find that it does indeed behave like a wave. If we design another experiment, in which light is supposed to behave like a particle, it sure enough behaves like a particle. So what really is the true nature of light? There is no simple answer to that question. It is all a matter of perception and expectation.

LIFE AS A COMEDY

In the same way, life can either be a comedy or a tragedy. And it's always in your power to determine how you want to see it. I prefer to see it as a comedy. And I highly recommend this to you, also. But let me explain exactly what I mean by that. I don't mean to suggest that life is a comedy like you see on television at 8 o'clock on channel 5. I'm using comedy according to the classical definition of the term—a progression from sadness to happiness, from a low point to a high point, from poverty to wealth, in every sense.

In literature, the best example of comedy is Dante's *Divine Comedy*. Although I don't believe there is a single joke in that entire work, it's a comedy in the sense that the story begins in hell and ends in paradise. Yet most people don't even know that Dante wrote two more volumes that take place after the completion of *The Inferno*. History has chosen to focus on the frightening, painful part of Dante's poem. And if you are not careful, you might find yourself doing the same thing in your own life.

Unfortunately, we live in a time that equates seriousness with intelligence, unhappiness with sensitivity, and victimization with moral authority.

We live in a time that has equated seriousness with intelligence, unhappiness with sensitivity, and victimization with moral authority. In short, we have largely chosen to see life as tragic rather than comic. But to the extent you participate in this, I believe you are limiting your potential for success. In the material sense, and even more importantly, you are doing nothing for your character. Or at least nothing good.

Humor can be your best tool for distancing yourself from the negativity and pessimism that's so rampant today. Granted, humor is not always an easy tool to use, but I believe its importance has been seriously underestimated as an element of strong character.

George Bernard Shaw said, "Everything is funny as long as it happens to someone else." But really strong people can laugh even when the joke is on them. Just as light conforms to various kinds of experiments, if you chose to find humor in life and in your own circumstances, you will find it.

If you're of strong enough character to see life as a comedy, in the sense I've described, you are strong enough to make it really be that way, as well.

And I am very serious about that.

7

FLEXIBILITY

An interesting article recently contrasted the history of the Ford Motor Company with that of General Motors. In the early day of the American car industry, Henry Ford's pioneering use of mass-production at the assembly line meant that Ford pretty much had things his own way. For years there was basically one kind of Ford car, the Model T. It was available in one color, black. You may have heard the famous remark old Henry Ford is supposed to have made, "The public can have any color Model T they want, as long as it is black."

Henry Ford had some great ideas about standardization and efficient production. But these same strengths revealed some vulnerabilities. Ford just wasn't very flexible. As long as he didn't have to be, all was well and good. Then along came General Motors. They started offering cars in lots of different colors and even began bringing out new and different models every year. Suddenly Ford, who had been making the rules, discovered that the rules had changed. The competition had changed the shape of the playing field.

Ford's success had been attained by limiting options and minimizing complications. But now there was immediately a need for adaptability and change. Despite its early lead in the car industry, Ford was now forced to play catch-up. It took nearly seventy years. That's what happens when rigidity and narrow thinking run into flexibility and creative innovation.

INEVITABLE CHANGE

Sometimes in the late afternoon, when the sun is setting, and I look out at the flow of traffic on our great interstate highway system, with the television picking up the five o'clock news of the world via satellite, and the telephone answering machine taking the calls, and supper cooking in the microwave oven, I like to reflect on how much the world has changed over the past fifty years. Microcomputers, supersonic passenger planes, moon walks, Israel and Egypt at peace, the collapse of communism, fax machines, video conferencing, and these are just a few changes I've seen in my lifetime.

My parents lived at the beginning of the 20th century and had to witness far greater changes even than I have. They saw the United States go from thirty-eight to fifty states, the horse and buggy replaced by the automobile, rail travel replaced by airplane travel, the candle and oil lamp give way to electricity in every home, indoor plumbing, the telephone, radio, and television. It must have been like being born on one planet and while completely wide-awake and going about their daily business, they were being effortlessly transported by some friendly alien to an entirely different and strange world. They were born in an age of the telegraph, railroad, and steamship. They saw the birth of the Atomic Age. Instead of fearing what might be west of the Mississippi, they learned that the entire human race could be wiped out by a single finger pushing the wrong button.

But perhaps I am not giving my parents enough credit. It's true they saw tremendous changes. The world of 1950 compared to the world at the start of the 20th century must have looked like a science fiction dream of the future come true. But not the way anybody would have predicted.

My parents not only lived with these tremendous changes, they also managed to thrive with them. They brought electricity into their home and change into their lives; they grew with the times. They welcomed the new. They didn't cling rigidly to the old ways, to the world they grew up with. They were flexible and put down deep roots and flourished. They were not frightened or paralyzed by the terrible promise of the powers unlocked by atomic energy. They believed in the good as well as in the terrible. They knew human nature and the will to survive.

They often told me when I was a little boy not to be frightened by all the big claims made by people in the world—after all, the human race was capable and adaptable. The will to survive was stronger than the will of any person or the power of any machine.

A strong character is not a rigid character. In fact, exactly the opposite is true. Although it's important to be firm when you know something is right and to maintain that right position even when the crowd is going against you and wants to put you down, it's also important to remember that no human being is God; nobody is infallible or invincible.

Sometimes when the tides have run against you for a long time, it may be that what you held as a certainty was, in fact, not true in the light of overwhelming circumstances. It's not only right, but it's also smart to be able to see more than one way to accomplish a task. It's wise to see more than one solution to any problem. It's a good skill to see things as someone else might see them. When the plan that served you so well for so long doesn't work anymore, it's time to find another way. It's time to bend. It's time to move on, to change, to compromise, to talk—or you will risk snapping like a dead branch in a stiff breeze.

TREE TRUTH

When it comes to lasting a long time, to standing tall and being strong but knowing when to bend, trees have a lot to teach us. If you have had first-hand experience of the tremendous destructive power of tropical-force storms, you know what change that can bring to an area, a community. I've experienced a hurricane and had a chance to witness close-up and personal what a combination of wind and water can do to everything that stands in its path. The rain fell so long and hard that it completely soaked the ground and loosened the roots of even the tallest trees. At the same time, the wind blew with such force that century-old trees, tall, and hard, and strong, were blown over like toy soldiers standing on parade knocked down by a toddler at play.

However, the enormous willows, some standing as tall as a house and covering what would be an entire lot in some parts of the city, were lithe, flexible, bending, and bowing gracefully to the slightest breeze or the mightiest gust. Each one weathered the heavy blows of the storm and almost the only large objects left standing after the air had cleared. Not only were tall trees, power poles, and sea walls crushed by the storm, houses built to stand up under normal circumstances collapsed and their roofs were carried off in one piece and blown into the next county. Everything that tried to oppose the storm's fury was damaged or destroyed. Everything that was strong yet flexible, survived.

Maybe you remember playing the game of Scissor, Stone, Paper when you were a kid. A refresher: You make a fist and count to three. At three, you put out a flat hand as paper; or you put out two fingers as scissors; or you keep the fist as a stone. To see who wins, scissors cut paper, paper covers stone, and stone breaks scissors. Whoever put out the winning object gets a point. The best strategy was not to stick with putting out the same thing. You had to try and guess what your opponent would offer and turn your fist into what would defeat your opponent's scissors, stone, or paper.

This game teaches a child to think about the nature of material. How something can be strong or appropriate in one situation, and yet be the wrong tool, a losing proposition, in another. It also teaches a child to vary approaches, to be flexible so the opponent can't anticipate the next move. As you are trying to outsmart the other guy, the other guy is also trying to outsmart you.

It remains to be seen how the great changes we are seeing right now, in our own day—computer watches, smart phones, the Internet, "tourism" flights on a space shuttle, the falling away of international boundaries to trade, the rise of nations in the Pacific Rim, and the apparent decline of European powers—will affect our own lives the lives of our children.

BE READY TO ADAPT

The nature of change is such that what today looks so large and important may turn out to be mere flashes in the historical pan—or breakthroughs that usher in a new reality. There is always something else we haven't even thought about. It could be something as obscure as a population explosion among virus-resistant rabbits in Australia that will be the key element in global change that we can neither anticipate nor imagine.

This has often happened throughout history and why all our best-laid plans do sometimes go astray. It's entirely possible, and even likely, that nothing will ever turn out as we expect. So no matter how much we prepare, one turn of fate can sneak up from our blind side when we are least expecting to be interrupted at our accustomed round.

When that time comes, as it will, the people who survive and even triumph over the unanticipated will be those who are ready to adapt. They will bend in the first gust. They will step out of the path of the charging bull. They will pivot while holding their place in the scheme of things. They will step back and let something else bear the brunt of the impact.

I don't really think it is less important or more important to be open to change and flexible in adapting to it than it has been in the past. It's always been important to be flexible and farsighted, anticipating whenever we can and when we can't, being prepared for all possibilities.

HISTORY LESSONS

The United States has been in existence for more than two hundred years. Think of all the things that have happened in that time. The immense technological and sociological changes that have taken place. The Founders deliberately left the Constitution a bit vague in some areas, so that future generations would have the flexibility to adapt it to changing circumstances. And that is exactly what happened. And it has worked for more than two centuries.

But now let's look back in time for a moment. The Roman Empire endured for about five hundred years—more than twice the time the United States has existed. The framers of the Constitution closely studied the decline and fall of Rome in order to create an American government that would avoid a similar fate. So far, their efforts certainly seem successful, but it will be another few hundred years before we can say we've lasted longer than Rome did.

Despite all the remarkable flexibility our form of government has displayed over the past two centuries, it's almost inconceivable that we will ever last as long as the ancient Egyptian empire, which spanned more than two thousand years.

Think of it. That is ten times as long as America has existed. Famines, floods, invasions, and plagues came and went. But through it all there was an unbroken succession of Egyptian Pharaohs. Nothing lasts that long, certainly not a government, without a great deal of flexibility.

Yet amazingly enough, when it comes to flexibility, and being able to adapt to the changing circumstances of history, Egypt isn't even the all-time champion. The oldest and longest-lasting empire in the world is that of the Chinese. Many dynasties, many emperors, many reigns, but always the empire endured. How is this possible? It wasn't because of military power or tremendous wealth, because over the course of thousands of years, those things came and went many times.

The real reason the Chinese empire lasted so long was because of the work of two very different philosophers.

The first, Confucius, provided ideas that became the solid foundation of the Imperial government. He supplied the theories by which the Imperial government was conducted. Confucius taught a code of ethics that provided specific instructions on how the ruling classes could fulfill their duty to the nation and maintain law and order. He was essentially a law-giver; a thinker who supplied some fixed beacons for navigating the ship of state into the unknown future.

The second philosopher, Laozi, had a very different perspective. Historians associate Laozi's ideas with magic and with mystical powers. But he also placed a very modern kind of emphasis on the need for intuition and the ability to react quickly to change. Laozi pointed out that sometimes it is best to advance by retreating. That sometimes wars can be won by losing a few battles. And long-term goals can be achieved by accepting short-term reversals.

Sometimes it is best to resist, like the tall grasses bending in the wind or like a river finding a new route around an obstacle. A powerful ocean wave smashing onto a beach may wash away a sand dune, but the individual grain of sand simply goes with the flow and is unharmed.

By incorporating both of these perspectives, the ancient Chinese emperor developed a structure similar to that of modern buildings in Los Angeles and Tokyo, which are built to withstand earthquakes. Their foundations are strongly reinforced, but there is also room for sway and give.

Flexibility is simple in theory and tremendously challenging in practice. It means we have to learn to distinguish between what we can control and what is beyond our control. Practicing flexibility requires great self-knowledge and iron-like self-control, as a master of the oriental martial arts. To be flexible does not mean to be weak, to flounder about aimlessly and confused because we think nothing can be done. No, it requires self-discipline. Flexibility requires a cool head, an appraising eye, poise, balance, and judgment.

INNER FLEXIBILITY, LONG-RANGE ADAPTABILITY

Up to now we have mostly talked about what can be called "tactical flexibility." Where a specific situation requires a knowledge of the various alternatives and a specific set of circumstances require nimbleness and dexterity. More difficult, and more important, is the inner flexibility and long-range adaptability that are called for from the person who wants not just to survive, but succeed.

A very wise man once said, "You can't step in the same river twice." Every moment, all things are changing, and the next minute is never like the last one. Whenever you achieve a hard-won success, it's always because you've been able to create a flexible response to the conflicting needs, ambitions, and feelings of other people. You've sidestepped the accidents of fate, the quirks of nature, and the innate tendency

Discern what can be controlled and what is beyond your control.

we all have to depend on yesterday's solutions to solve today's problems.

I mentioned how the Founders relied on the example of Rome as they constructed the framework of American democracy. It is interesting to observe that at one of the times of greatest luxury and power, and perhaps complacency ever in the history of the world, the heyday of the Roman empire, a philosophy arose that attempted to teach these men who ruled the known world how to govern themselves.

SELF-MEASUREMENT BENEFITS

These philosophers, who called themselves Stoics, taught that to simply survive in life, let alone be a leader, you must learn to take responsibility for the way things affect you. At the same time, you must learn to bend with the wind of forces too great for your control. This kind of self-measurement and self-control should be part of every grown-up's character. After all, adults are the leaders of their own family, their children who grow up, in part, learning from their example. To be firm but fair; to be clear and consistent but flexible is to possess maturity.

Kids are delightful, but sometimes they are the most inflexible people on earth. Since circumstances almost never turn out exactly the way they want them to, they are on a constant roller-coaster ride in terms of their responses; up one minute, down the next. One young lady, a little girl of five, actually, will only eat her morning Corn Flakes a certain way. If the parent doesn't pour exactly one-half cup of whole milk straight from the refrigerator into the bottom of the cereal bowl, and then add the Corn Flakes so that they float on top of the milk, and then sprinkle a teaspoon of white sugar over that, she won't eat breakfast at all, not anything. She could be hungry, cranky, and weak, but she will purse her lips together and shake her head so hard that her braids whip her cheeks. She will not eat.

In other ways, however, because they haven't formed opinions about a lot of things and lack the experience that can trick people into anticipating an outcome, kids can be far more adaptable than grownups. They can accept poverty, harsh living conditions, or sudden reverses in fortune. For children, all things look equally inevitable and have always been there. Children have softer bones and dispositions than older people, so they're more apt to receive new impressions instead of repelling or opposing them.

YOUNG AND OLD, TRAITS AND GIFTS

Like all our traits and gifts, both can be blessings and curses. Old people can get set in their ways and can be mentally as well as physically brittle. They can tell themselves that they know it all and have seen it all before. They struggle against the hardening of the arteries and the ossification of ideas, becoming as stubborn and willful as children who don't know anything. And often with the same harmful results.

When I think about an older person who has managed to adapt to life's changes, big and small, and stay ahead and keep in step, I think about that grand old vaudevillian, cigar-smoking joker and singer, and admirer of beautiful women—George Burns. George Burns started out in show business before the days of "talking pictures." He toured the vaudeville stage circuit with his wife and comedy partner, Gracie Allen. Together they joked their way from the stage to the movies and the radio. Later when television came along, the George Burns and Gracie Allen show was one of the great ones. Running every week for years and years.

Until one day, Gracie Allen died leaving George Burns alone in the world with only his cigar, a trunk full of gag-lines, a few million dollars in the bank, and a lot of great memories. Did Burns retire after his wife's death? Did he crawl off and play golf until the Grim Reaper came for him? No. Burns wrote himself a new act, a new set of monologues. He made a new career in the movies and basically reinvented himself. He continued to crack jokes and pursue lucrative movie and television roles and personal appearances. He made a career out of being old. And he didn't do that by being inflexible, you can bet.

I mentioned earlier about the little girl who would only eat a certain way. Old people, too often, get fussy about their food too. They also require feeding and sometimes even diapering. It's uncomfortable to think about our bodies turning on us this way, but it doesn't do to be rigid and set our minds into some hardened position that we can't accept help when it's needed and offered. That kind of pride destroys a person just as surely as walking into speeding traffic saying to yourself, *The pedestrian has the right of way.* True, but tell that to the ambulance attendant.

FLEXIBILITY AND COMPROMISE

Flexibility and compromise are at the center of democracy and the American way of life. In private life, there are places where you can be unyielding if you want to be and only you will profit or suffer because of your firmness. In the national arena of politics, however, with so many groups holding so many different and often uncompromising positions, the only way for the government to work is to declare all things are negotiable. They must talk everything out to find some path acceptable to all parties, if not satisfactory to any of them.

That is why the Founders, when they drew up the Constitution of the United States, made religion and government completely separate. You can't compromise in matters of religion; you'd be a hypocrite or worse if you did. So the Founders set off to the side all the things where people really can't be expected to compromise—for theatres other than political theatres; for contests other than public policy.

There was an American statesman, Henry Clay of Kentucky, who was known as the Great Pacifier and the Great Compromiser. Clay served in the United States Senate, in Congress, and was Secretary of State under President John Quincy Adams. Clay both incited the War of 1812 and helped negotiate the Treaty of Ghent, which settled the war. Pursuing a consistent policy of reconciling the conflicting interests of the nation during the time of the Great Westward Expansion, Clay ramrodded the Missouri Compromise and helped enact the national road.

As a presidential candidate, Henry Clay said that he would rather be right than be president. And he certainly never did become president. Whether or not he was right, I couldn't say, but I suppose he felt that he was right. And that right meant finding a common path to an agreed-upon end.

A wise and flexible old gentleman used to dine every month in his club downtown. Sitting at a long table, covered with a white linen tablecloth and silver candlesticks, and served by tuxedoed waiters, he loved to regale companions with the fruits of his many years of experience. After dessert and coffee were served, he would push back from the table and light an enormous imported cigar. "This cigar is the only indulgence of an old man," he would say with a chuckle, as he struck the wooden match against his thumbnail, then he would launch into one of his stories.

The story usually began with a question, such as, "Did I ever tell you about the time when I was setting up factories for the giant XYZ Corporation in the backwoods of Georgia?" He was compelled to teach them a little lesson in business and good manners. Although the stories always started out the same, no two stories were ever alike. And there would always be a wealth of wisdom, through example, a veritable motherload of remarkable instruction.

This man who was so old and so wise and so flexible had one iron-clad rule for dealing with other people—never be the first to break a bargain and always assume that what happened before should not happen again. He said, "If a man fools me once, I think, 'That's not nice.' And I remember it. And if the same man fools me a second time, I think, 'Shame on you.' If the same fellow tricks me a third time, well, I have been warned and should have changed my ways and didn't. So I think, 'Shame on me.'"

Here's a little rhyme to remind you of this wisdom: "Fool me one, that's not nice. Fool me two, shame on you. Fool me three, shame on me." If you're not changing your responses to the situations and circumstances that make up your life, you're not being flexible—you are throwing away your greatest asset as an individual human being.

No one can completely control external events—but we can always control and adapt our responses. No one can know which cards fate is going to deal out—but we can always control how we play them.

8

PATIENCE

Suppose for a minute that you know exactly what you want to accomplish in life: you know you want to get a good education; you want to have a successful career; you know you want to make some profitable investments; you know you want to raise a family and have your children turn out well. You may even know how you want to go about achieving these objectives. You may have it all planned out in great detail. All that is very important. All that is very good—but is it enough? I'm afraid not.

Let's suppose there's a vast, hugely powerful force that nobody can withstand. And this immense force is always active and in furious motion; it never rests. It's like a slowly flowing river that can eventually carve the Grand Canyon out of solid rock. But that comparison doesn't really do it justice. The force I'm talking about is much more formidable than any river or ocean or glacier or any other natural phenomenon.

In trying to achieve your life's goals, would you prefer to fight against this great force? Would you want to struggle against this mighty power that has all the odds overwhelmingly in its favor? Or would you rather enlist this great power in your cause and make the inevitable work *for* you instead of *against* you?

Take your time before answering. Think it over. By the way, *time* is that great power I'm talking about. Time is the mightiest force in the world or even the universe. Of course the answer to the question I posed is very obvious. Why would you ever choose to fight time when you could have time on your side? Who wouldn't want to harness the great river of time that flows through all of life? Why wouldn't you want to use the power of time to generate power in every area of your existence? To turn the turbines of your hopes and dreams, to charge your every aspiration with lightning bolts of electricity?

MAKE TIME WORK FOR YOU

There is only one way to make time work for you, and that's with patience. There has been talk in the news lately about changes in the climate, global warming, and so forth. And how the level of the seas will rise during the coming years and put whole communities underwater that now stand high and dry.

All I can tell you is that in certain parts of the country it has been plenty hot and dry the last few summers. And I'm sure there have been times when the residents of those areas would have liked to have seen some big ocean wave come rolling across the plains. Think for a moment about any state that is in the middle of this continent, away from the coast, and ponder this question: What do you suppose it would take to turn that state into a kind of surfer's paradise? So when it gets hot you could just go out and let the waves cool you off.

For example, what would you need to turn Texas into California? If you take the perspective of an engineer, you'd maybe think about the water rights, the dams, and all the good stuff you'd need. The kind of undertaking that would make the Hoover Dam and Lake Meade look like a little inflatable backyard swimming pool. From that perspective, the whole notion is not only impractical, it's also impossible. But if you believe everything that has been written and said about global warming and rising water, you realize that it isn't really an impossible proposition. In fact, some people say it's inevitable. You don't need any water rights or dams to see it happen, all you need is patience.

Here is another illustration of the power of patience. Imagine you are at a cottage in New England when a blizzard hits. There's more snow in less time than any other winter on record. If you went to bed in the middle of this blizzard, you'd probably assume that when you got up, you'd have to shovel the drifts away from the front door just to get down the steps. You may even think about getting started on the work before you go to bed.

But in this case, as it turns out, all that bedtime effort wouldn't have been necessary. Overnight, the wind keeps blowing, and while you sleep it shifts around one hundred and eighty degrees. So all the snow on your front porch is cleared away naturally. You don't have to knock yourself out with a shovel. You may be saving yourself from a stiff back or a heart attack. And all you had to do was wait.

Patience. There's a type of person for whom everything is undertaken out of a desire to achieve a goal. They prepare food to eat it, not just for the fun of being in the kitchen. They start a business to make money. They exercise to get in shape. I'm sure that some of these people are very successful and certainly highly organized. But in my opinion, a person of truly strong character sees success as an adventure, not as a point with an estimated time of arrival.

The latter approach, to me, is impatient thinking. Impatient thinking can lead a person into some very big mistakes. First of all, when you are always looking somewhere else, whether it is down the road, up toward the mountaintop, or off toward the left-field fence where you are hoping to hit that grand-slam homerun, when you're looking off in the distance like that, you often miss what is under your very own nose. That means the pleasure and fun of living that comes in the here and now is overlooked for something that not only isn't here yet but may never arrive.

True patience is more than just a waiting game. Patience doesn't mean you sit around hoping for something to happen. Patience is not a passive quality. Sometimes patience

Patience is not a passive quality.

can mean doing something else entirely—thinking about another venture, taking off in a different direction while you give events a chance to run their course.

Throughout his long career on the screen, John Wayne never felt he got the credit and recognition he deserved for his skills as an actor. Yes, his films were consistently successful at the box office. And even today John Wayne is still the number one favorite movie actor in the United States. But a big following among movie-goers didn't translate into critical esteem or the respect of his peers. That's what the Duke wanted. And he felt he deserved it, too.

Then in the last years of his life, he made the movie *True Grit,* in which he played a drunken one-eyed old U.S. Marshall named Rooster Cogburn. That portrayal got John Wayne the Oscar he had been waiting for forty years to receive. It wasn't the kind of high-and-mighty hero role he'd played when he was young that finally got him his award, yet it was a role that he'd waited for all his life—and he didn't even know it was coming.

A colleague of mine told me this story. He was traveling across the country on a speaking tour and found himself delayed in Chicago while changing planes. In the first-class traveler's lounge, he fell into conversation with a gentleman who actually looked a bit like John Wayne during his *True Grit* period. He was a little surprised to learn this gentleman was actually from New York City. And there was another surprise. Despite his rough-hewn appearance, this fellow traveler proved to be extremely soft-spoken. His favorite pastime was playing chess.

But as he talked about his experiences in the construction business in New York City, he also demonstrated that he carried a big stick. His company had developed some of the most important commercial real estate in Manhattan. As successful people always do when they encounter other successful individuals, my colleague asked him how he had done it.

"Well," he said, "after I got my engineering degree, I spent some years getting hands-on experience in construction. I didn't want to be supervising people in any job that I didn't know how to do myself. Later on when I started putting together my own projects, I had to deal with some pretty tough street-wise operators—cement company guys, building inspectors, trucking companies—but I never tried to pretend I was any kind of hard case myself. I used to tell them right up front, you play straight with me and I'll play straight with you. I never tried to take advantage of anybody. But I never let anyone take advantage of me either. You see, I always was and I still am, a great counter-puncher."

The man continued, "Anybody who takes a shot at me in business had better make sure it's a good one. Because I'm going to hit back hard. It's like chess. You don't necessarily hit back right away. You have to be patient. You have to wait for the right moment. You have to let the other guy know, 'Okay, you had your chance, next time it's my turn.' But you don't say that out loud. You don't say what you've got in mind. And you don't say when it might be coming. You just go on, polite and friendly as ever. You don't ever let on that you're waiting for an opening. But you rest assured that your chance will come. It's like any other investment, it takes patience. Patience is the key."

Needless to say, those several hours between flights were both informative and enjoyable for my colleague. We can learn from this story. Don't concentrate on things you can't influence, like when the planes are going to take off. Instead, focus on things you can control. And when you meet some-body you can learn from, then learn everything you can while you have the chance. You never know when you are going to come across a book or an article that will provide a piece of information that can transform your life.

One thing is for sure, however, and I've said this many times, the book you don't read isn't going to help. It's the same with meeting people. You never know who is going to teach you exactly what you need to know. Even if you don't need to know it now, you might need to know it at some point in the future. That may not be for fifteen years—but it might just be in fifteen minutes, too.

SOWING AND REAPING

A number of years ago there was a movie titled *Being There*. It was the story of a not-very-bright man who worked all of his life as a gardener. But through a series of comical coinci-dences, he became an advisor to the President of the United States. Whenever the president asked the gardener his opin-ion on anything, he answered in terms of what he knew, which of course, was gardening. But the president wouldn't realize that he was talking about gardening. Instead, the president was sure he was speaking in metaphors and allegories; that he was making wise analogies between the world of nature and the world of human affairs.

Now, I value straight-speaking as much as the next man, maybe more than the next man. I don't want to take up your time with figures of speech that might belong to a poem, play, or movie. But with respect to the topic of patience and its role in building a strong character, I do think that gardens have lessons to teach us all. Lessons about sowing and reaping, about tending and keeping.

For example, there is a story about W.C. Fields, the Hollywood comedian of many years ago. Fields bought himself an unusual type of cactus called a Century Plant because it blooms so rarely that it seems like it only happens once every one hundred years. Although, in fact, the time is much shorter. Anyway, Fields had purchased the Century Plant from a florist who was either misinformed or not entirely honest because he told the comedian that the Century Plant was just about to burst into bloom. And wasn't that an exciting thing! It apparently excited W.C. Fields, because the notoriously cheap comedian agreed to pay top dollar for the rare treat of seeing the Century Plant produce a flower.

Fields invited all of his friends over to his house to witness the historic event. The company arrived, food and drink were served, and all eyes were on the plant. But no flower was forthcoming. Finally, outraged and embarrassed by the uncooperative cactus, Fields took a riding crop and began to furiously thrash the plant all the while he was shouting, "Bloom! You fool, bloom!"

There are a lot of times when you can try anything you want to hurry things up, but things just aren't going to hurry. In fact, there's only one thing that works—patience.

IMPATIENCE

It's strange, but young people have a much more difficult time with patience than people who have more experience in the world. It seems like the older people get, the more able they are to wait—despite the fact that sometimes they have considerably less time to wait in. You could argue that older people ought to learn how to act quickly, decisively. While younger people need to learn how to wait. When young, you have just about all the time in the world and you just can't wait to use it. For a young person to have patience is a rare and powerful thing.

How can we explain that impatience of the young? Maybe it's because when you are a teenager or in your early twenties, one year seems like a very long time because there are milestones to reach—driving a car, graduating, getting a job, finding a mate. Five years seems like forever. And ten years is almost more than you can possibly imagine. But more mature individuals can actually look back ten, twenty, or even thirty years and use the knowledge they have gained to create patience and a sense of perspective.

At the risk of confusing you, I'm going to make what may sound like a contradictory statement: "A patient person is always richer than an impatient one. Even if the patient person has less money." What do I mean by that statement? Riches and wealth can take other forms besides dollars and cents. Okay, that sounds good, so, in what sense is the patient person richer?

The actual answer is very simple. A patient person is always richer than the impatient one because the patient person can always afford to wait. The patient person is never desperate and has time to spare. While the person in a hurry is always on the verge of bankruptcy as far as time is concerned. In any situation you can think of, impatience is a source of weakness and fear, while patience is substance and strength.

Another way patience gives the person who has it an incalculable advantage over the person who doesn't is that it gives him deeper insight into him or herself and others, which is a mark of great character. If you can only see the short-term, if you can only think in terms of the here and now, then you are like a person with only one eye. You can't judge distances. You live in a world that is flat and two-dimensional.

PATIENCE AND PERSPECTIVE

In other words, the impatient person lacks all sense of perspective. Perspective lets you measure your plans and current events against things that have already occurred and also against your desires and aspirations for the future. Then and now, here and there, near and far, need and know,

Patience equates to substance and strength.

watch and wait—these are the dual optics that allow the patient person to see in stereo. Where the near-sighted person sees only the present or the dreamer sees only an imaginary future; and more likely than not, trips over mistakes trying to get there.

The history of the 20th century can tell us a great deal about the value of patience and perspective. History proved that time is the strongest ally you can possibly have. No matter what the odds against you or the level of adversity you're facing, time gives strength to those who have it on their side.

This truth was very convincingly demonstrated over the course of World War II. Germany had enormous successes in the early years of the war with the blitzkrieg; the surprise lightning strike from the air and land without warning that was used first against Poland, and later against the countries of Western Europe. Japan also used surprise attacks successfully and almost gained a decisive advantage with the treacherous bombing of the unsuspecting American fleet at Pearl Harbor. The nations allied against Germany and Japan knew that time was on their side and they were prepared to be patient.

Although you won't find this discussed in many history books, one of the most important events of World War II actually took place right here in the United States a few months before the attack on Pearl Harbor. At that time, the U.S. Army held a series of massive military exercises in Louisiana designed to assess the preparedness of the American forces for participation in the war that was spreading around the globe. As it happened, the war games in Louisiana revealed glaring deficiencies in our military preparedness. It quickly became obvious to our military commanders that if America was soon drawn into the war, as many believed it would be, there would have to be a long period of rebuilding and modernization. This would have to take place at the same time as American forces would be fighting worldwide with inferior and outdated equipment. And that is exactly what happened.

It took almost three years of patience, hard work, and sacrifice before the U.S. war machine was brought up to modern standards. But President Franklin D. Roosevelt and generals including Dwight Eisenhower and Douglas MacArthur knew that the wait would be well worthwhile and once the modernization was completed, victory would be assured.

On the other side of the Atlantic, it was much the same story. Winston Churchill knew that England would have to endure months and years of bombing and threats of invasion. But he also knew that time was on his side. With great patience and courage, the British people waited out the bombing raid by planes and rockets. At last the tide began to turn, and the world realized that patience and endurance were going to defeat the most devastating attacks that had ever been seen up to that time.

In Russia too, the city of Leningrad was under siege for more than a year. But the Russians knew the value of patience perhaps better than anyone else. More than a century earlier, after all, they had let their bitter climate and the sheer size of their land defeat the French armies under Napoleon—the same natural forces eventually prevailed against the new invaders. Because of their patience, the United States, England, and Russia won the Second World War against enemies who banked on surprise and the hope of a quick victory.

PATIENCE AND CHILDREN

There's no area of human activity that requires more patience than raising children. If you don't have patience when you start out in this endeavor, you will learn it one way or the other. A baby is born after nine months. If the future mother is tired of pregnancy before that time, too bad. And when the child does arrive, he or she grows and develops at a pace that is quite beyond the parent's control.

Parents who try to force a child's development are asking for trouble—one point on which psychology and common sense are in complete agreement. We've all heard of parents who think they can create another Einstein by giving their two-year-old a book on astrophysics. Or that if a child is made to play the piano for an hour a day, it will bring about the second coming of Mozart. None of this works, of course. It also ignores the fact that all real prodigies develop completely according to their own timetable. Even then, the result was usually not exactly what one might have hoped for. Mozart, for example, had a very difficult later life and he died young. In part, because he grew up so much sooner than other children. He never really had a childhood; at thirty he was already an old man.

It doesn't take textbooks on physics, hours of music, or any other kind of force to teach something effectively to children. It just takes one thing—patience. It may seem like a calloused comparison, but there is a sense in which raising children is like any other investment. So much depends on when you need to cash in your chips. If you are in a hurry, if you need to see results tomorrow, you're putting a lot of pressure on everybody and there is likely to be a great deal of disappointment.

But if you can afford to wait, you can ride out the hard times and eventually realize a profit.

The odd thing is, sometimes waiting for years is easier than it is to wait for a few days or even a few minutes. None of us felt too strained because we had to wait twelve years to go through grammar school, middle school, and high school before graduating. Or at least the first eleven and one-half years didn't strain my patience. But ask me to wait forty-five minutes for a plane flight, or twenty minutes in the waiting room of a dentist's office; and if you catch me on the wrong day, it is almost more than I can handle. We all find ways to wait for the next paycheck. But how many can wait patiently in a check-out line in a crowded supermarket? How many people can stand and wait quietly for an overdue train on a railroad platform?

TWO KINDS OF PATIENCE

It's as though there are two kinds of patience. The kind that sets you up for the long term, and gives you the promise of a better and richer day after tomorrow. Then there's the other kind. The sort of patience that helps you remain sane and sociable while you are waiting in line or watching the clock or waiting for a pot of water to boil. These kinds of patience, so different and yet so much the same, are nailed into your character and have a fundamental effect on your nature.

Any doctor will tell you, it's better for you and anyone around you if you don't get exasperated about little things. If you don't fly off the handle at every annoyance and stick in your way, your blood pressure remains low and your friends and neighbors remain happy. Greet life's little problems with calmness and patience. Almost all problems can be solved if only you take the time to see them and think them through. That is very easy to understand and very easy to say, but it takes a strong character to put into practice.

I'm never sure what to think when people say, "I want to make a million dollars by the time I'm forty." Or, "I want to retire by the age of forty-five." This combination of goals plus deadlines strikes me as short-sighted and maybe even a bit naïve—it takes a worthwhile goal and subjects it to a supposed timetable. While you might have an idea of what a million dollars would mean to you, or you might have really exciting plans for your life after you hang up your work clothes, I don't see how people can reasonably expect to know who or what they will be, think, or feel at some arbitrary moment in the future.

This kind of thinking misses the whole point of success. The real payoff in financial and worldly success isn't the result of an amount of money divided by the age you are when you get it, or some other actuarial formula. The real payoff is found in the qualities of character you develop along the way.

There's a story about a young man who had a very old and rich uncle. When the uncle died, the young man was called to the office of his attorney and told that he had been left a huge fortune. To collect it, however, he first had to run a certain errand, which was described on a slip of paper. It seemed simple enough. But when the young man tried to accomplish it, the first task turned into another and then another. As he pursued his uncle's final request, the young man was led into foreign lands and exotic adventures and untold dangers.

More years passed and the young man nearly lost track of how and even why he was on this long journey. He could hardly imagine what its end might be. At last the odyssey led him back into the very same lawyer's office where it had begun. "I'm here to collect my inheritance," said the heir; no longer a young man but a much wiser one. The lawyer smiled, "As your uncle intended, you've already collected it, in the places you've been and the things you've learned. And again, as he intended, it will last you for a lifetime."

Success that comes too easily or too quickly almost never lasts. For people who achieve that kind of success, there is always a lurking feeling that they haven't really earned it. And that feeling eats away at their character. If they're lucky and smart, they create some new challenge for themselves in a totally unfamiliar field. These people have to build their character to survive their sudden good fortune—that's the kind of

Success that comes too easily or too quickly almost never lasts.

character built in an emergency. In fact, it is a true case of the cart coming before the horse. This doesn't require patience, because there is no waiting, planning, or even expectation involved. It's more a test of a person's upbringing than a test of character.

We've seen how often the qualities of a strong character demand the presence of opposite qualities in an almost paradoxical way. Patience is no exception. Patience does not mean wait until next year, it means this year; but if not, next year for sure. I think Thomas Edison put it best, "Everything comes to him who waits. But it comes sooner to him who hustles while he's waiting."

There's a way of putting your best effort into something but detaching yourself from the outcome. That is the essence of what patience means. It's not at all like wanting to make a certain amount of money by a certain age or winning the game before the clock runs out. The real point is to keep the clock running. The real way to win is to stay in the game for as long as it darn well takes.

9

CONFIDENCE

Confidence is such an important quality of strong character. It is really a form of optimism, a certainty that things are going to turn out the way you want and that you have the power to make that happen. Confidence is also one of the most elusive and misunderstood qualities of a strong character.

How do we recognize a confident individual? Is it someone who dresses well, has a firm handshake, a shoeshine, and an intense smile? Perhaps, but more than any other quality, I think confidence is found to a greater degree in what we give to others than in what we have within or about ourselves.

The root of the word "confidence" is "confide." Confide is a compound word derived from the Latin language meaning "with and trust or faith." When someone is sincere in a business deal, when an offer is made and real money stands behind it, when someone makes a promise and means to keep it, we call it a bona fide offer, a good-faith offer. Music played on a top-of-the-line audio system is said to be high-fidelity. Meaning faithful to the sound made by the live performer and instrument at the time and place of the recording. At Christmastime one of the carols children sing is the old *Adeste Fideles, Come All Ye Faithful*, to instill the confidence and good faith of the season.

Confidence has to do with inspiring trust, which you can only do by having faith in other people. Confidence enables you to walk into a room full of strangers and converse with anyone without fear. Confidence imparts poise and bearing. It makes the strangers in that room think, *Here is someone I not only can talk to, here's someone I want to talk to.* Ill-at-ease people make everyone around them ill-at-ease. Feeling right makes others feel right, and they in turn give back what's inside them—the very confidence that you give out. It's like sounding an A note for an orchestra. Every instrument with an A-string answers in sympathetic vibration. Confidence is the right note. And other people's confidence is the sympathetic vibration.

Confidence is a form of optimism.

Confidence makes people want to believe what you say to them, want to accept you as you present yourself.

Confidence is more than something that passes between two individuals on their way through the day or through their lives. Confidence is the entire basis of social order. It's the foundation of our monetary system. Think about it. The dollar bill has imprinted on it, "In God We Trust." We have confidence that the government stands behind the value of a dollar. We are confident that the infrastructure and manufacturing capabilities and market-drive of consumers will be there tomorrow as it is today.

We are confident that all things are growing, not fading. And so, we buy and sell stocks, trade futures, invest in industry. Consumer confidence gives the goods that confident truckers have driven to market, a place to go. Get them to the shelves and people will buy, no matter what. That's the spirit of global enterprise.

It's not based on gold, it's not based on material possessions—it's based on trust and confidence. Without the good-faith confidence of other people, trading partners, bankers, the earnest intention of buyers, and the credit of merchandisers, the whole system of world economy, along with all of the governments of the world would collapse. What would be left? Nothing! Except for the early barbarism of rule by brute strength and physical intimidation.

Confidence is a powerful force that can grow in power and flurry if given the right environment.

Truly confident people's belief in themselves is strong enough to believe in others. Conversely, distrust in yourself breeds distrust in everyone you meet. A confident person gives you the confidence to create confidence in others. The strength of your character makes you a stronger character. The questions here are: How do I develop confidence? How do I learn to believe in myself so that others will believe in me, too?

CONFIDENCE IN HUMAN NATURE

George Washington was the commander of the American army during our War of Independence from Great Britain. Why did the Continental Congress ask Washington to lead the troops? And how could he—a landowner and surveyor, and formally loyal subject to King George of England—find the strength and confidence to ask his fellow colonists to lay down their lives fighting seasoned troops of the greatest army of the richest, most powerful nation of the world? Although Washington was a British subject, his roots were in America, the world he knew and loved, the land that gave him his life was here, not in England.

As a youth, Washington had traveled with the British army surveying unmapped territories in the New World, while England fought the French and Indian War. So, Washington had firsthand knowledge of both the terrain where he had to fight and of the enemy he would oppose. And because he traveled with the army as a surveyor rather than an officer, George Washington knew the temperament of the men he would actually have to fight.

George Washington understood that with fortitude, patience, and confidence in the justness of the colonial cause, his little army could and would prevail, largely through his ability to impart his own inner confidence to the men fighting under him. George Washington of Virginia was not only able to win the war against the Redcoats, but was also to be called the father of his country as the first president.

No amount of historical debunking from his time to now has managed to tarnish the image he has left us. George Washington still inspires confidence, and his face is found on that one piece of paper that has the respect of the entire world, the American dollar bill. I venture to say that the face on that paper inspires the confidence, rather than the number on the bill giving value to the face.

In the past two hundred years, a great expression of confidence in human nature, the goodness of humans, the confidence, the meaning, and the value of a person's vision and integrity can be found in two men: Brigham Young and Pablo Picasso. Two very different men. One, Brigham Young, a man of religious inspiration led his people out from persecution and abuse into a promised land flowing with milk and honey. A promised land where no one had been able to see a paradise before.

And the other is the artist of all ages, Pablo Picasso. A young boy growing up in Spain at the end of the nineteenth century, Pablo Picasso completely revolutionized what is meant by the word "art." Over a life that lasted more than ninety years, Picasso set forth a steady stream of paintings, sculptures, drawings, and writings, while loving many women and fathering numerous children right up to the very end of his nonstop creative existence.

Think about the first time you came across a painting by Picasso; if you're truthful about it, you probably have to admit you just didn't get it. The faces with all those sharp angles and strange colors. Both eyes are on the same side of the face like some kind of flounder fish that you could catch with worms and lives on the bottom in the sand. But if you went back and looked at his pictures again, you likely started to see how they made a kind of sense. In essence, you were learning from this man, to see differently. To understand how there could be two sides to a person's face, for example, that would show up at the same time.

This artist had so much confidence in what he saw and was so strong and clear, and even generous in showing the rest of the world what he saw. He taught everybody to see the old world in a new way. And because of his confidence, we can all become a little more confident ourselves, and learn not to reject new things out of hand, just because we can't recognize them at first.

Picasso was generous because he made a lot of art but he also made a lot of money—the confidence he felt in his art translated into confidence in art dealers. And confidence on the part of the art buyer's market and the auction market. This, in turn, translated into confidence on the part of large corporations and super-rich investors, in the lasting value of Pablo Picasso's vision of the world.

It's not uncommon to stand in the museum and listen to other people say things about modern art, such as, "My kid could do better." Or, "What's the big deal?" Or, "I don't get it." And you know, a lot of stuff that's passed off as art deserves these kinds of remarks. In that sense, the art market is a big confidence game. But the amazing thing is the confidence game can only be played because there's such a thing as real art that has lasting value, and everybody hopes that the thing they are sitting in front of might fit that bill. And when the artist is real, like Picasso is real, his signature is as good as the

U.S. Mint. And even a little drawing can be cashed in for many, many dollar bills.

It's hard to think about political and religious leaders, like Brigham Young, as having something basic in common with a great artist like Pablo Picasso. But they are inspirers of vision and confidence in the people who follow them. Brigham Young, at least, looked at the landscape of the United States of America, at the barren desert of what is now the prosperous State of Utah, and saw that the cactus and alkali flats held the promised land. The Great Salt Lake, just like the Dead Sea in the State of Israel was, in fact, the land of milk and honey.

The Mormons—the people Brigham Young led from western New York State all the way to Salt Lake City where they built their tabernacle—were universally feared, hated, and despised. They were lynched, beaten, and denied the right to practice their religion openly. Their religion— which came to their prophet, Joseph Smith, in his home in Rochester, New York—compelled them to seek peace. To seek a place on this continent where they could live in harmony among themselves and with none to persecute them. So they set out, suffering all the way, despised by all, and battered by the elements.

Joseph Smith, the prophet, had died. It fell to Brigham Young to be their Moses and lead them. He led them with vision and with confidence in the power of justice and the rightness of their cause. He couldn't offer an immediate reward, money, or the kind of power that comes from controlling industries or markets, but he did offer each and every person who marched with him, the power of self-respect and self-command. The power of right to win out over wrong. The power of justice over law and the power of confidence over the forces of ignorance.

In fact, if you travel to Salt Lake City today, you see a prosperous, modern metropolis. Travel to any major city in this country and you'll see a skyscraper built and owned by the Church of the Latter-day Saints. Those same Mormons who settled in a desert valley with nothing but the little they carried with them and their faith. All the outward attributes of inner confidence flowed to them because their confidence was real and enduring.

Brigham Young's was a kind of politics that deals with the way we feel about ourselves and about others. And about how we treat others and expect them to treat us. And while you may not agree with the Mormon's religious philosophy, you have to respect the dedication that led them to their present condition. They followed the politics of trust—the confidence we talked about earlier when discussing the economy.

The other kind of politics as usual, which has to do with awarding contracts and building roads, dams, and essential services, can only function when the government has the trust and respect of the citizens. It's hard to say which is the chicken and which is the egg here; but without people helping each other, you can't even make scrambled eggs much less have a chicken in every pot.

BELIEF IN YOURSELF

"Alright," you say. "All this history makes a fine story; I'm convinced I want in. But I don't have the strength of George Washington, the faith of Brigham Young, the imagination of

Pablo Picasso, heck, I don't even have a law degree or good connections in the county highway department. How can I achieve this level of belief in myself?"

I think I can give some very specific answers to your question. If you have read this far and want to know more, it means I've earned your confidence. And remember, you can't inspire confidence or feel confident in yourself, if you can't feel confident in others. So in a real sense, the first important step has already been taken and you are already on your way to a new world of confidence. Let's venture a little farther down this path we are standing on, looking ahead together.

There are three areas we have to talk about before you are ready to add confidence to the other building blocks of your unshakable character. Those three are: *First,* developing the quality of inspiring confidence by uncovering your own confidence in who you are and how you were raised. *Second,* seeing how you can derive confidence from that formal education and training you have received and the characteristics of your teachers and mentors. And *third,* drawing confidence from the challenges and experiences you've had in all areas of your life and the success you've had in dealing with it. Let's look at each of these areas one by one.

First, developing the quality of inspiring confidence by uncovering your own confidence in who you are and how you were raised. To grow up at all means you have certain kinds of vital equipment that are necessary to survive in this tough, technical, highly developed world of ours. Your parents taught you basic skills—how to walk, how to eat, and later feed yourself, and later what to feed yourself, and perhaps good manners. You were given a certain amount of physical strength and mental endowment. Maybe you aren't a rocket scientist, but maybe you know how to fix a lawnmower—something many rocket scientists can't do. Maybe you don't have a degree in accounting, but you can tell a joke so well that the whole room will roar with laughter.

What are your strong points? You have some or you wouldn't have made it this far. Maybe you can save money. Maybe you know how to fix things. Chances are, you not only have a personal strength—a gift, talent, ability that should be a source of pride and give you real confidence—but it's possible that you take it so for granted that you don't realize what it's worth. Your talent and skill are what you may take for granted and maybe don't value enough. Talent isn't hard work, it's a snap.

Second, seeing how you can derive confidence from that formal education and training you have received and the characteristics of your teachers and mentors. If you grew up in the United States, you attended school and more than likely have a high school education. Because almost everybody has a high school education, why should you take confidence in my diploma? In reality, not everybody has earned that diploma. The United States is one of the few countries in the world where almost everyone can read and write and do math. So we take for granted that in the backwoods of nowhere a diploma would probably qualify you to be president, king, or the big boss. So boss, don't sell that sheepskin short because you have it. You wouldn't think of it as nothing if you didn't have one.

Also, your teachers and mentors who showed you the ropes in class, at the first job, or the new place saw something in you that you maybe didn't see yourself. Want to know what that something is exactly? If you can pinpoint what they gave you and showed you, you will see yourself through the eyes of that other person, that teacher, mentor, or newfound friend. What they give you is what they see in you already; invisible to yourself. If they didn't see that you were capable of running that machine, taking that order, landing that account, making that sale just as they were capable, they wouldn't have bothered to teach you in the first place. They had confidence in abilities that you may not have known you had. And they shared that confidence with you because you already had the skill or only needed the sharing.

Third, drawing confidence from the challenges and experiences you've had in all areas of your life and the success you've had in dealing with it. The last one is even more important than where you were born and who your parents are, and whether or not you went to any school or the right school, and whether or not anyone stood by you and showed you the ropes. You have lived and you are here, so you have the richest bank to draw upon that there is, you have experience.

You may have traveled around the world, you may have known many people and learned the ways of other lands and other languages. Or you may have experienced life in the same place among people you've known all your life and known them in the way that no one on the move forever dealing with new faces and new friends can ever know another person. That's your bankroll. That's where you can learn and draw from with confidence.

The thing about experience is that it really works for you. I'm sure you have some confidence in life because you are reading this book; and perhaps you're even getting that sympathetic vibration, which is the confident tone that sounds in all of us.

A CONFIDENCE (CON MAN/WOMAN)

The "confident" man or woman is someone we all admire. Someone we all want to emulate, and rightly so. On the other hand, a "confidence man" (con man/woman, con artist, swindler) is someone quite different.

During a business lunch in the Wall Street area, a colleague of mine had been approached by a stranger with a highly attractive, apparently very lucrative business proposition. This out-of-the-blue proposal had all of the marks of being bona fide, genuine—letterhead, seed capital, articles of incorporation, a board of advisors.

The man making the proposition had been active in government operations overseas in some capacity that none of his current associates could actually explain. This former public servant intimated that the opportunity involved buying shares in a corporation set up to import and export fresh fruits and vegetables from Central and South America, outside of the North American growing season: apples in April, plums in December, lettuce in February. However, under the cover of these fruits and vegetables, they would actually be selling weapons to both sides of a civil war in a medium-sized Latin American quasi-democracy, which was and is against the law.

My friend stepped away from his lunch table to place one phone call to a man who would know about such dealings. Sure enough, this very individual had been accepting investments from wealthy individuals across the country, without ever showing his books. Furthermore, so the plan ran, investors would be invited to inspect the foreign warehouses where the goods were stored, and then held for sizeable ransom from their families, friends, and business associates. Can you imagine what kind of person would attempt to play such a trick on someone who knows his way around? We must be keenly aware of people who try to promote confidence in shady dealings—truly con men and women.

You have to learn to crawl before you can walk and walk before you can run. Nobody grows to be an adult in this day and age without the leap of faith, the act of confidence that says, "I have the confidence and maturity to share my talents and skills with people. I have the goodwill and the sharp eye to do well and to do more than just survive." I assure you that when you have confidence in others, you are sensing your own strength. When they sense the confidence you have in yourself, they can do nothing to harm you. What others have, you also have. But what others may lack, you don't have to do without.

You can be absolutely confident of that.

10

GOOD HEALTH

What is good health? Is it a matter of opinion or a matter of fact? Is it a style? Or is it rather the substance of what we are as human beings? Is it the condition of the physical plant, if we think of ourselves as flesh and blood machines? Or the state of our emotional being, if we think of ourselves as more thought than matter? And in what sense is it an element of strong character?

You thought health was all about the body, didn't you?

A very wise older lady once told me, "If you have your health you have everything. Lose your health and there isn't enough money in all of the world to make life good or to make you feel like life is worth living." I didn't completely believe her when she attempted to give me the benefit of her long experience. After all, I was just a boy. Like most young people today, I thought that feeling good and having all the parts of my body in good working order was something that came with the territory. Like everything else, it just seemed to happen by itself almost every day of the year. I could take it for granted and I did.

But at the point in life I am now, there have been times when I've been sick and wondered, *What would happen if*

I were to lose my health? Would that be a test of character? I certainly think it would. It's a test of character when you get the flu over a weekend and you want to just lie there and complain. But instead, you lie there and quietly watch television. Or at least it seems to be a test of character until it's over and you forget about it.

But something like that, a minor illness, is really more like a tap on the shoulder than a test of character. You feel the little tap, you look around and nothing is there. Whatever it was, it's gone already. But sooner or later it will be back. Someday there will be more than a little tap on the shoulder. Someday you will look around and whatever it is won't be gone yet, not by a long shot. It tests your character a little just to think about that, doesn't it? But I'm not trying to scare you. I'm just trying to dramatize a point.

You know the kind of life you live when you are a kid. You can eat anything and you do. If you drink beer on the tailgate of your buddy's station wagon on the night of the high school football game, you can drink as much as you want, maybe more than you want, in fact. In college, you stay up for all-night cram sessions fueled by coffee and donuts, the radio, and perhaps cigarettes, unfiltered ones at least in my day. Looking back on it now, it all makes sense. You're feeling yourself getting bigger and stronger every day. And that's the only real evidence you've got to go on. So why not just go for it? After all, it hasn't hurt you so far.

Of course, the reality isn't quite that simple. But it's not as simple as thinking that just because you're older, things are now going in the opposite direction. And that while you used to want to do everything, you should now want to do nothing. No, reality is by no means that simple either.

There's a saying I heard in church about the same time that wise old lady told me that when you have your health you have everything. It took me just about as long to understand that saying as it did to figure out what good health really means to people. The saying was, "You have to lose your life in order to find it." You have to lose one way of living to find a different way—one that is better suited to who you are at this particular time. You can do that, though it takes character.

I've been very fortunate. I've never really been sick. It has dawned on me by now that good health is more than just the absence of illness, it's more than just not being sick. Good health is the direct result of right thinking and right living. In other words, of strong character.

DEVELOP A HEALTHY ATTITUDE

A buddy told me about his football coach who always told the boys on the team that the most important thing they could do for themselves, as a team playing football and as individuals playing the game of life, was to develop what he referred to as a "healthy attitude." Sure they had to do push-ups, tackle a dummy, and push the blocking sled. But if they didn't do it with a healthy attitude, then as far as this coach was concerned, they were just so much dead weight pushing around just so much more dead weight.

When I heard what the coach said and his emphasis on having a healthy attitude made me thinking that good health was different from just a strong body, it had something to do with character as well.

A *healthy attitude* is knowing that to go from point A to point B you have to walk a straight line and not veer away or get distracted by what might seem pleasant for a moment, but really don't contribute to your well-being. Or as the coach might have said, "To the good of the team that is depending on you, you have to go straight up and down the field. You can't go sideways just because the hot dogs and soda pop and the cheerleaders are over there. That sort of distraction is for after the game, if ever. And not being able to keep to the task is unhealthy thinking, and bad attitude, and weak character."

I used to think that all of that was cornball stuff. I still think it is cornball, but also important and even true. Your attitude, the slant you put on things, the way you lean into life or back away from it is all part of your character. And if you're in life for the long run, you need strength and endurance for that— which also derives, in part, from your character, at least when you get past the age of seventeen or eighteen. To live a long time and be well throughout, you have to be an athlete of health, a real long-distance runner. Anyone who has ever even just watched the Olympics on television knows that character is an important part of running.

While health may have never seemed like a quality of character to you, I hope you are starting to see that it truly is one. It's hard to think clearly, to feel confident, strong, decisive, and wise if you are short of breath when you stand up after a long spell of sitting down in a chair, to cite an extreme example. To cite examples that are less extreme: How can you hope to make the right decision about where to go with your career, what to buy and what to sell, approach a new client, or call on your old friend if your pants are too tight or the middle button keeps popping open on your shirt?

EVERYTHING IN MODERATION

But here's the good news. I say you don't have to believe every scare story that comes over the news and television telling you not to eat this or that because of what statistics say has happened in X number of cases. You don't have to make yourself crazy because of what too much of something tasty or greasy or sweet does to laboratory rats. You don't have to become a health fanatic to understand that some things in large amounts really aren't good for you.

A Greek philosopher of the Classic Age said, "We should all do all things in moderation and nothing in excess." That's a principle you should definitely apply to your lifestyle. It can't hurt to have an ice cream cone now and then, a little sweet to reward you for a job well done. A little something to take the sour taste out of your mouth on a bad day. But don't go gobbling ice cream by the quart and follow up with a pack of cigarettes and a fifth of rye whiskey. There are people who do just that, and it's a one-way ticket to the wrecker's yard. So is driving yourself crazy about health, however. So remember the principle, "Moderation in all things, nothing to excess."

Worry and stress are as bad for your heart as a high cholesterol count, which has been proven pretty convincingly. A long-term study in Finland included two groups of men who were asked to follow very different diets over a period of years. The first group could eat and drink anything they wanted. Let the chips fall where they may. The second group was watched closely, everything they ate was recorded and evaluated. No eggs, butter, or cheese, no coffee just herbal tea, no meat, but macrobiotic pasta was permissible. Which group had more casualties? You make the call.

What's worse is to have a high cholesterol count and always be worrying about it and punishing yourself for it with a sheet of strict Puritan rules. It's much easier to just follow moderation in all things. That way health really is a function of character rather than the calculator. Yes, go easy on the food and drink, go easy on the rules, too.

Take, for example, the man who was a real fitness nut, even before it was really popular. Every day he did his free-weight workout, then he ran five miles. Every day he ate the right foods, every day for twenty-five years, from the time he was eighteen until he was forty-three, he drank a glass of carrot juice and watched the nightly business report on his exercycle. That was where he died of a heart attack at forty-three.

There's also the experience of a wealthy woman who became a follower of a man who preached long life and perfect health through diet. She gave him large amounts of money and faithfully adhered to all his food-related instructions until he died, at an early age. She never again allowed his name to be mentioned in her presence. That may be why I've forgotten his name. Although, not the poetic justice of his passing on.

A doctor friend of mine, a cardiologist, a man of good judgment who is very unlikely to be swayed by fads and fashions in health care or anything else, explained it all to me this way: "You have to understand who you are and how you are made." In other words, you have to understand your character, physical, mental, and emotional. Not everybody is made to run a marathon, climb mountains, or play defensive tackle for the Chicago Bears. Not everybody has the physical or mental equipment to be a truck driver, rocket scientist, or in sales. Each of these careers involve different levels of activity. These people live in worlds with different customs, different ways of training and thinking, and different ways of celebrating.

A rocket scientist doesn't need to do twenty miles of road work every day. A truck driver doesn't need to sit still and read the small print under a lamp for hours at a stretch. A football player doesn't have to stay up all night driving through heavy downpours on the vast stretches of the mid-West interstates. These people tax their bodies in different ways. They all need to eat and relax in different ways, too. One person might enjoy jogging, another playing the piano, and another swimming.

Whatever the particulars of your physical nature and what-ever the condition of your character, there is one thing I can say immediately and with complete assurance: If you are seriously out of shape and engaging in behaviors that are bla-tantly self-destructive, you're going to find it very difficult to respect yourself and will make it nearly impossible for others to respect you. This is just a fact of life in today's world and in today's system of value.

ADOPT A HEALTHY LIFESTYLE

Recently I saw an obviously wealthy man pull up at the entrance of his country club in a limousine. He needed two flunkies to pry him out of the car. Even the valet guys exchanged smirking glances. If you want success, if you want to lead, and if you were anything less than a success-oriented individual whose ambitions are not going to be held back by the hand that fate has dealt, or the place that fortune finds you, you must embrace a healthy lifestyle.

Being in good physical shape is a big part of good health. There was a famous woman in the world of fashion who said, "You can't be too rich, or too thin." That was twenty-plus years ago. And now it may be you still can't be too rich, but the other part of the saying would have to be, "Or have too much muscle definition." I could be wrong about this though. I base my informal research on what the most popular film actors look like in any given year.

A young woman of my acquaintance was close to thirty, and well, a bit of a marshmallow. She smoked a little, ate what she pleased, and never gave too much thought to her looks, which she was losing, or her health because she still had it. Then one day the doctor told this young mother of two that she had a heart condition. She was informed that she would have to take pills for the rest of her life and never exert herself again. No strenuous sports, no excitement, no unnecessary stress. Though she was not even at the beginning of middle age, she was sentenced to a spectator's seat at the games of life.

She thought about what the doctors told her for a few days. Looked at her children and hugged them, and friends. And decided that enough was enough. Just what was it supposed to mean to be alive? She threw away the pills, changed her diet, started lifting weights, and took long vigorous walks in the mornings. She toned up, she bought a new wardrobe, and joined the workforce. Five years after she was told by medical science that her active life was over, this picture of health now enjoys a successful executive-level career in the burgeoning and fast-moving field of computers and information science.

Good health raises your esteem, your standing, and respect in the eyes of other people. Good health may give your character and ambition every advantage and put you in the way of the good things in life that come along. But all these things do not exhaust the benefits of good health. Despite the great and certain worldly rewards for staying healthy and fit, they are not the sole or even main reason to embrace the habits of good health.

If I can be allowed a moment of philosophical reflection, the greatest benefits to health are found in the mind, spirit, and soul, of the seeker. *Hold on a minute,* you are thinking. *Are you going to go fuzzy and mystical?* No. I'm here to talk sense, not treat, or push vitamins. And in fact, if there were one formula, one answer to the question of what is the true path to good health, if I knew what that answer was, I would hold the key to the most vexing problem of the ages. And this book would be the basis of a religion, not a practical guide to building strong character and achieving success.

Good health may really be an effect of character as much as a cause of it. In my opinion, being a person of strong character is the best prescription for a sound mind and a sound body. If you feel good about yourself, you will naturally want to take care of your body. But if you lose respect for your body, you're more likely to become slip-shod in other areas, too.

HEALTHY EATING

When it comes to digestion, there are certain foods that help the plumbing work smoothly. But those foods alone don't make for a healthy and balanced diet. You need variety in your diet to fulfill your body's many nutritional needs. It's likewise very beneficial and important to have variety in your life. What's true of financial health is also true of physical well-being. If you keep doing exactly what you've been doing, you'll keep having exactly what you have.

Anybody who does the same thing every day, year in and year out, with no break or vacation, is probably in no position to know if he or she is in good shape. As discussed earlier, you can't know what you have until you leave it, or lose it, or get something else. Probably the easiest and most helpful way to break up your day and keep the biological clock wound up so that it doesn't run down in the middle of the best days of your life, which is today, is to catch a nap whenever the opportunity presents itself.

"But I stopped taking naps when I graduated from kindergarten," you may object.

And I ask you, "Have you been better off because of that?" What does every CEO of any major corporation have in the office, right there, across from the big desk, with its leather upholstered tilted back swivel chair? A couch. "And what do you suppose that couch is for?" It's to have a little snooze before addressing the board about the latest attempt at a hostile takeover, or the upcoming stockholder's meeting.

Remember, every dream is a vacation. And Shakespeare himself said, "Sleep knits up the raveled sleeve of care." John Kennedy kept to his scheduled naps even through the Cuban Missile Crisis in 1962. Did this save the world from nuclear catastrophe? Well, something saved it.

There's a saying that comes down to us from classical time; it's in Latin, of course: *men sana in corpore sano.* What does it mean? Word for word it means, "A healthy mind in a healthy body." That's the ancient Roman prescription for living the good life, smart life, and feeling good and smart about yourself.

You just can't sharpen your mind like a pencil so it comes to a fine point, it always gets shorter and shorter until it is worn down to a stub and has to be discarded. Neither can you just eat, drink, party, and fight without a thought in the world. Or so the Romans believed during their glory days. And I agree with that line of thinking. Later in the declining days of the empire, the Romans forgot their own advice. And soon the decline became a fall. I'm sure the message is clear.

For centuries, the people of China have absorbed wave upon wave of conquering barbarians into the vast reaches of their country. Always the invader seized control of the government. But then a curious thing happened, and happens every time to the conquering hoards. After a few years of rule, the Chinese don't become barbarians, but the barbarians become Chinese. Part of the reason for the ability of the Chinese people to swallow up and digest the armies that would rule them has to do with the country being so large and so old. Part of it has to do with the philosophy and the wisdom

A healthy mind in a healthy body.

of this mighty nation, which has for many thousands of years made a science of good health and long life. It's the national character, you might say.

One form of the martial arts that centers on self-defense is an art called *tai chi,* which combines physical exercises with philosophy and diet. It teaches a person to defend himself or herself from all kinds of attacks. Attacks from hostile people using weapons and surprise or brute strength attacks from within the physical body, in the form of disease—even attacks in the form of destructive emotions including anger and fear. Character and chemistry are both taken into account. I'm not going mystical on you, I'm just following my philosophy of learning things wherever I can.

I've heard of a very old Chinese man who lived an odd but astonishing long life. He ate very little, exercised regularly, and kept a turtle in his bathtub. The turtle, he explained, was a symbol of longevity, and it gave him an example to follow in his dealing with the world—slow and steady. And it supplied

A turtle in your bathtub?

a certain kind of undemanding companionship in what must have been at times, a lonely life.

There is much more to be said about health, but there are a few hard and fast conclusions to be reached thus far. I think health is an aspect of character because I see evidence that ethical people are happier and more relaxed. Stress on the other hand, which I associate with hostility and anger, is said to cause physical problems. I happen to believe that people get what they deserve, however—and perhaps they get even a little bit more.

So there is really no end to talking about health. And there shouldn't be, because health is about going on, about continuing for as long as you can. It's not about stopping. What's healthy is persisting as far and as long as you can. Maybe speeding up or pausing along the way. Maybe taking a side path sometimes instead of staying on the beaten path.

Staying healthy is the only way to get the good part from all the parts of life. It's the way you stay strong. The way you stay interesting is when the mind and body meet.

In a sense, good health is what all the hard work is about. It's when the heart, mind, and muscle cooperate. The expression *in the flower of youth*—and that flower includes the bloom of health.

11

ACHIEVEMENT

I believe success comes with character, and success builds character. I don't believe, as apparently some people still do, that suffering and defeat are necessary for developing the soul. I know they're not good for the body or the mind. Failure doesn't make you feel better either mentally or physically.

Of course, it's an inevitable part of life and you'd do yourself a favor by taking the opportunity to learn from your failures—but I think there's no point in banging your head against the wall once you realize it hurts. I don't mean to sound hard-hearted, but I believe if you reach a certain age and you haven't achieved much in your own terms, you can't ascribe this to bad luck, a difficult childhood, or any other external factor. I personally feel that your strength of character does come into question at that point.

And let me make it clear that your definition of success may be different from the next person. I'm not implying that you need to have a fat bank account or a Rolls-Royce to be successful. But if having those things is integral to your definition of success, then that is what you should be aiming for.

A MAN NAMED STEVE

Let me illustrate what I mean by describing the philosophy of a very successful and interesting man named Steve. Although he was still in his mid-forties, he had already founded a very profitable advertising firm in the Midwest. He sold it to one of the country's largest agencies for roughly three times his company's annual growth. So, he had become a very wealthy man and had plenty of years left to enjoy it.

During a discussion with some friends of his, the topic turned to the career problems of a mutual acquaintance. A man of obvious intelligence who had an MBA from one of the most prestigious universities in the country. His high level of ambition had led him to strike out on his own as soon as he earned his business degree. But now, fifteen years had passed. His consulting firm was still hard-pressed to pay the rent on his office. Oddly, he still continued to impress everyone who met him as an extremely sharp all-around businessman. He read the *Wall Street Journal* every day. He knew the names of all the CEOs of the major corporations. Talk to him for five minutes, and you would think he was a real player in the business world. But he had never made any money.

Steve's friends were confused by the whole idea of a good businessman who has never had success in making money. They felt it was like saying someone was a great baseball player, but he strikes out all of the time and makes a lot of errors. Steve thought about this for a minute and then offered his perspective. "In the business arena, I believe *achievement* is a prerequisite for calling someone successful. You can't be a good businessman and never make any money. A good tree bears fruit. If it doesn't, it's not a good tree." I think Steve's analysis is right on the mark for a certain segment of the business arena.

In certain professions, one of the highest goals you can achieve is to generate income for the company and thereby fatten your own bank account. In those businesses, success is measured by money, plain and simple. So if you are in that type of profession and you haven't made money, you probably should take some steps to strengthen your character.

In other words, character isn't an abstraction that exists somewhere up in the sky divorced from the real world. There may be other things you should do also, but you should certainly do some soul searching and some character development.

THE MEASURE OF ACHIEVEMENT

But let's broaden the scope of the discussion a bit, and look beyond business success. I've already said that in my opinion, you need a strong character to make money. And that if you haven't made money, your character very likely needs work.

But I also want to stress my belief that it takes character to achieve success in any form. Whether it's in the business world or anywhere else. There are some people who just aren't interested in making a lot of money. I'm not one of them, but I can see their point of view. For these people, achievement is measured in terms that aren't so easily quantified.

There was once a small dinner party in a beautiful home located in the hunt country of New Jersey. The host was heir to a fortune that began when his grandfather invented the first milking machine. But he had long since distanced himself from anything that at all smacked of life on the farm. He was primarily an investor now. Though he and his wife were also very involved with philanthropic activities.

177

On this particular evening, they had convened a gathering of successful people from several different walks of life, providing a vivid example of what winners have in common regardless of their particular field of endeavor.

In attendance, was a prominent attorney, an investment banker, and an owner of one of the largest automobile importing businesses in the country. Each accompanied by their wives. The person who dominated the conversation was a slightly built, impeccably attired gentleman from New York City who spoke with a mysterious European accent. He was known only by the host.

From the beginning, the topic of conversation for the evening seemed to be opera. Those who were present were clearly eager to take advantage of this fellow's presence and listened respectfully as he discoursed on his favorite subject. Neither the attorney, nor the car importer, nor the banker were what you'd call opera aficionados. Their wives didn't seem very knowledgeable about arias either.

It was just something about the personal magnetism of the slightly built fellow. There was a genuinely charismatic quality that made everyone want to hear what he had to say, even on a subject that might be remote from their own interests. He spoke mostly about the Metropolitan Opera in New York City, though there were allusions to Milan and Paris. With regard to the Met, he offered detailed critiques of all of the previous season's performances as well as his impressions of individual singers. This was followed by views from behind the scenes that made it clear that this man held some administrative position with the Metropolitan Opera itself. He definitely wasn't just somebody who bought a ticket. Names of significant benefactors of the opera came up, prominent individuals in the business community. It was clear that this dapper little man was on a first-name basis with these people.

Then after holding forth for well over an hour, he suddenly seemed to grow tired and with profuse apologies, he informed them that he would be leaving. There were protestations from those present, but the slightly built man explained that he really had no choice. There was a matinee at the opera the following day, he would have things to do, and he really couldn't afford to be at anything less than his best. "So, what can I do?" he said with a sigh, a little smile, and an exaggerated shrug in the European manner. And a moment later he was gone.

There was a quiet moment after he departed, a void that would have to be filled. By this time, the guests had all moved from the dining room to the library where a dessert wine was being served. Finally, one person in attendance took it upon himself to ask what exactly it was that the departed guest did at the Metropolitan Opera? Was he the person who scheduled the program? Probably years in advance. Was he the person who made the creative decisions? Shall we do a little light opera here and then a big tragic one there? Or was he more involved with the business end of things? The person who negotiated with the artist's agent, and put his foot down financially when somebody started getting too big for their britches?

After a moment's hesitation, the host answered the question. "Well," he said, "that man who just captivated us for two hours, that gifted raconteur, who had just held us spellbound with tales of divas and maestros is the same man who runs the coat check room at the Metropolitan Opera. During the performances themselves, of course, no coats are being checked, so he is free to slip into the back of the hall and listen. I bet, to this day, he has heard every note that has been sung or played at the Metropolitan Opera in the last twenty years."

HIS OWN MAN

In all the years that I've observed, studied, and pondered the laws of success and the variations of human character, I don't believe I've ever heard a better example of self-possession and aplomb than that man. As he left that night, every guest had pictured him as returning home to an elegant Park Avenue apartment. Now they had to substitute a one-bedroom apartment in an outlying district of the city, or maybe even a furnished room someplace. There was no way to know for sure since none of the guests had any idea what they paid the man who ran the coat check room. But what did it matter? He was his own man. He had truly achieved that. And how many people could say as much regardless of their income or net worth?

You've probably come across many people who provide a very different kind of example. People who really let the air out of the balloon. This tends to happen more often as individuals move into middle-age. You can recognize them on the street. They walk along with their head down, moving at a snail's pace. When I talk about developing character, these people don't know where to begin. As they see it, it is pretty hard to focus on character when you have credit card payments to make and a hundred other things to worry about.

Well, here's my opinion. If these people had given a bit more thought to building a strong character over the years, maybe their credit card payments would be a little more manageable at this point. But it's never too late, according to Aristotle. Fifty-two is the age at which a man's philosophy is fully formed. But it's okay to run a little behind schedule, as long as you recognize it and do something about it.

AN ANT'S PHILOSOPHY

You don't need volumes of books or the library to create a personal philosophy that will help you to achieve your goal. You can do that anywhere. You can do it right now. In fact, we can do ourselves a favor by developing the philosophy of an ant. There are at least two reasons why ants are unique and important. For one thing, an ant always knows where it wants to go, and it keeps trying to find a way of getting there, no matter what. If you put a pebble in front of an ant, the first thing it does is try to find a way around the pebble. It tries to go one way, if it can't get around there, it tries to go the other way.

If it still can't get around, it tries to climb over the pebble. And if for some reason it can't climb over the pebble, it will try to lift the pebble, even though the pebble may be hundreds of times larger than the ant itself. And if it finds it can't lift the pebble, it will look for other ants to help. And if all the ants working together can't lift the pebble, they will finally start digging a tunnel underneath it. And even if that doesn't work, they will literally start to gnaw their way through the pebble. How long will they keep trying? Until they die. Because the one thing they will never do is quit. That's the ant's philosophy of achievement. And we may want to incorporate it into our view of the world.

The other reason ants are important is because of what they do in the summer. During the summer ants plan for the winter. They don't have any credit cards; they don't use the present moment to create debts and liabilities for themselves and the future. They use the present moment to create assets for themselves. Do you remember the fable about the ant and the grasshopper? The grasshopper laughed at the ant for working so hard all summer. The grasshopper just enjoyed himself, leaping around in the high grass without a care in the world. When the winter came he starved to death, while the ant had plenty to eat. Everyone has been a grasshopper at some point in our lives, just make sure you are not one now.

Character is the means for transforming ideas into achievement. It's somewhat abstract in the sense you can't lay your hand on it, point to it, or weigh it on a scale—but in a very real sense, character is what allows you to get where you want to go.

Character transforms ideas into achievement.

ANALOGS OF CHARACTER

If you want to drive from your home to a store on the other side of town, you need an automobile with gas in the tank and keys to start the car. You also need to know how to drive and judgment based on life experience to tell you when to step on the brakes if the traffic light changes to red. You need a true intention to reach your destination so you don't stop for coffee and a piece of pie every ten minutes.

You need to know how much time to allot so you can return home in time for whatever else you have to do. And you need enough maturity to call and say you'll be late if you get stuck in a traffic jam. You can't lay your hand on any of those things and you can't measure them with a yardstick. But they are as important to reaching your destination as a car, the gas, and the keys to start the engine. They are analogs of character.

Let's continue this comparison for another moment or two. There are all sorts of ways to keep track of the condition of a motor vehicle. You can look at the tires to see if they have worn out their tread. You can look at the odometer to see how long it has been since you changed the oil. And you can turn on a switch and then walk around the car to see if the headlights and the taillights are working properly. There are objective indicators of the condition of your car.

EVALUATING YOUR ACHIEVEMENT

Similarly, there are ways of objectively evaluating your achievement. Most people don't take advantage of them as often as they should, but they are available nonetheless. For example, you can put together a financial statement to determine your net worth. You can hire an appraiser to learn the market value of your house. You can compare where you were ten years ago to where you are now to determine the degree of progress you have made in your life.

As I've tried to explain, achievement depends on character in the same way that a successful drive to the grocery store depends on knowing when to apply the brakes and when to step on the gas. But how can you know if your character is in good enough shape to get you where you want to go? To continue the metaphor we have been using, there are ways of discovering whether you still know how to drive without having an accident. I believe there are ways of evaluating the strength of your character that are almost as accurate as determining the depth of tread on a tire or amount of gasoline in the tank of a vehicle.

In order to use these techniques for character evaluation, all you need is a commitment to be ruthlessly honest with yourself. At first, that kind of ruthless honesty may include a little bit of pain. But once you accept the fact that character is basic to achievement, you'll gladly pay the price. Just as the gas gauge of a car indicates full and empty, with several demarcations in between, you can learn whether your character has enough fuel to get you to your life's destination. You can learn to tell whether you are on full or empty, or somewhere in between.

While a car runs on only one fuel that is indicated by a single gauge, character, in my opinion, can be evaluated by four different imaginary gauges. Here's the first one, on the right-hand side of the gauge, corresponding to the letter *F* for *Full* on a gas gauge, I want you to imagine the letter *R,* which stands for *Refusal*. And on the left side of that gauge, imagine the letter *C*, which stands for *Complacency*. If your character is good and strong, there are things that you refuse to accept in yourself or in other people. In your work, you refuse to accept anything less than your best effort.

That doesn't mean that everything will always work out as you hoped and intended. But that's not the point. There will always be variables you can't control, but your effort level should always be maxed out, regardless. With your family, your commitment should be just as strong, you should refuse to compromise in any area where your family's needs and welfare are concerned. And in your personal life, you should similarly refuse to accept pettiness, dishonesty, or unethical behavior in any form. That's the right-hand side of the first character evaluation gauge.

On the left-hand is the letter *C*, which stands for *Complacency*. But it could also be the letters *L IS* standing for *Let It Slide,* or even *WTDA* for *What's The Difference Anyway?* Ask yourself where you stand on that scale. Do you have enough good, strong refusal to achieve what you want to achieve? If not, it's time to make a pitstop right now.

The second character reading gauge has the letter *D* for *Decision* on the right. On the left is the letter *M* for *Maybe*. Ask yourself, are you a person who comes to a fork in the road and turns right or left? Or do you stop the car, scratch your chin and say, "Maybe I'll go this way, and then again, maybe I'll go that way." And in the end, you go nowhere.

Think about the big issues facing you and your life right now. It could be that you want to leave your job and start a business of your own. It could be that you want to get married. In any case, are you the kind of person who comes to a decision and puts it into action? Or are you someone who says, "Well, maybe, but then again, maybe not"?

Now imagine a gauge with a *W* on one side and an *A* on the other side. The *W* should be in bright red or orange, while the *A* should probably be a dingy green or pale yellow. That's because the *W* stands for *Want,* as in *I Want it Now,* or *I Want it Real Bad,* or *I Want it so Much I'll Do Whatever it Takes.* The *W* means you'll go to law school for five years at night while working full-time during the day because you want to be a lawyer. The *W* means you'll get up at four o'clock in the morning every day to work on your novel because you want to be a writer. It means you'll travel from one end of the country to the other to find the doctor who can make your child well. I know people who have done all those things because they wanted something—and eventually they got it.

The *A* stands for *Apathy,* that's when you really don't care what happens. And if you really don't care what happens, it's just as well because it certainly isn't going to be anything good.

Now we come to the last of our imaginary character gauges. On the right-hand side is the letter *P* that stands for *Promise.* And on the left-hand side is the letter *F* that stands for *Fear.* If you are a person of strong character, you will promise yourself to achieve your goals. You never consider the possibility of not achieving your goals. You have made a promise and you're going to keep it. When you set out to drive to the grocery store, you don't stop at the doorway and think, "What will I do if I don't make it?" You simply intend to get to the grocery store, you know you are going to get there, you will get there, it's simply assumed.

Fear is simply the inability to make a promise to yourself. It kicks in when you start thinking about all the bad things that

Strength of character is the foundation of achievement.

can happen to you on the way to your destination. And before long you're thinking, *Wouldn't it be easier just to stay home? Isn't it safer to just stay in bed? Isn't it better to pull the covers up over my head?*

In this discussion, we've been using the metaphor of going across town in a car. Let me conclude by referring to another little excursion. It's one that I know for a fact you have already taken. When you were learning how to walk, you made a silent promise to yourself that you were going to do it. It may have been scary at times, you surely stumbled again and again, tears surely fell from your eyes, but no matter. You didn't even think about that. Each time you fell, you forgot about it as soon as you regained your feet. Because you had promised yourself you were going to walk across the room, you did it! How long did it take? Who cares? You did it!

At that point in your life, you had the strength of character to overcome fear and keep the promise you made to yourself. Do you still have that strength? Whether you realize it or not, you do. When you were that little child we've been talking about, you asked yourself, "How long am I going to work to realize my dream of walking across the room?" And you instinctively answered, "As long as it takes."

Make that same promise to yourself right now. Making it takes strength of character. And as I've tried to show, strength of character is the foundation of achievement. I can promise you that.

12

STRONG CHARACTER

One of the most remarkable books ever written is titled *Coming Out of the Ice* by Victor Herman who passed on a few years ago. It's an autobiographical account of the author's struggle to survive during fourteen years in a series of Siberian prison camps; all of them located in the far north near the Arctic Circle during the years of the Stalinist regime and the Soviet Union. In the first few pages of the book, by way of introducing himself, Herman declares that he is one of the toughest men on the planet, if not *the* toughest. And whether or not you are prepared to take his word for it now, as he tells you so, he is absolutely sure you will agree with him by the time you finish the book.

And he is right. By the time you've finished the book, you'll know that over the course of these few hundred pages, you've been in the company of the toughest man on earth. Physically, mentally, and spiritually. This is definitely a man with a very strong body and a strong character to go with it. Victor Herman had been born in Michigan but he had moved to Russia during the 1930s when his father went there to work in a factory built by the Ford Motor Company.

Herman, who was in his early twenties at the time, was arrested for being politically unreliable and was sent to Siberia. The philosophy of the Soviet Prison System at the time was very simple: prisoners were simply worked to death. In the Arctic cold of the Siberian winters and the mosquito-infested unbearably humid summer, the camp inmates were given one impossible task after another with inadequate clothing, impossibly poor equipment, and almost no food. Faced with this kind of existence, a prisoner would inevitably lose his will to live and death would occur not long afterward.

Victor Herman was an amazing exception to this rule. Though he had no real hope of a life outside the camp, though he had nothing to live for in the sense that most of us are used to, something inside him refused to be broken—just out of sheer stubbornness, just out of sheer strength of character.

At one point a special task was arranged for Herman, something the camp administrators were certain that he wouldn't survive. Early one frozen morning he was sent out into the forest with only a single guard accompanying him. And there he was shown several dozen full-size trees that had been cut down and stripped of their branches so that they could be used as telephone poles. He was then ordered to single-handedly load the trees onto some railroad flatcars before the end of the day. It was literally an impossible task, like something out of a fairy tale or a bad dream.

But Victor Herman did it. Somehow he did it. Simply because he refused to be beaten or give up. It was a miracle, but it actually happened. It was a feat that dwarfed any Olympic athlete. And as it happened, Victor Herman was in an excellent position to make that particular judgment. Because after his release from the camp, in the 1950s, he became coach of the Soviet Olympic Boxing Team.

The author of *Coming out of the Ice* performed many heroic feats during his years in Siberia, but he considered the incident with the telephone poles to be his masterpiece. As he worked he was watched by only the armed guard, who just stood there silently throughout the day probably half frozen himself. Undoubtedly the guard was completely dumbfounded by what was happening before his very eyes. When the impossible job was finished, Victor Herman could not resist walking up to the guard and throwing his arms around him. This incredible display of physical and mental toughness simply had to be celebrated somehow. Even if only with a Russian prison guard in the middle of a vast Siberian forest. As Herman described it, the guard allowed him a brief smile.

And then the two men trudged back to the camp where Herman endured many more years of incarceration before his eventual release, his remarkable Olympic career, and finally his return to the United States after almost thirty years in the Soviet Union.

Victor Herman's amazing story certainly deserves to be told. And I believe that there is a great deal to be learned from his accomplishment. But it is not what you might think. I'm not going to suggest that you can be like Victor Herman or that you should even try. In fact, I think the value and the extraordinary power of his story lie largely in the differences between what this man accomplished and what we can expect of ourselves.

SELF-MOTIVATION

To me, the most amazing fact about Victor Herman's survival is the fact that he found motivation entirely within himself. Nobody cared whether he lived or died. He had no reason to think he would ever have a life outside the prison camps. It was made obvious to him throughout every minute of every day that his captors were simply waiting for him to give in and growing more and more impatient about it all the time. To me, the fact that Herman managed to maintain his will to live under these conditions of total isolation is even more amazing than the things he accomplished with his body.

Very few people are able to develop this kind of intrinsic motivation. It's an axiom of human nature that most of us, virtually all of us in fact, need reasons outside of ourselves to accomplish anything of significance. We can still be people of strong character, but we need something outside ourselves to help us become as strong as we can be. Just sort of wanting to be financially successful is rarely enough to make it happen. Just wanting to learn a new skill, give up a self-destructive habit, or make some other major change in your lifestyle usually won't cut the mustard.

But what if you had to get a large amount of money to afford the very best medical care for someone you loved? What if you had to learn how to speak a new language to save a family member who had been imprisoned in a foreign country? Or if you had to change your way of living to find a way out of some other life or death situation? Your motivation would move to a much higher level. If you're like most people, *having to* is a lot stronger than *wanting to*. But often, and especially when you're young, that difference isn't always clear until someone points it out to you.

In my own life, it was my mentor, the late Earl Shoaff, who pointed out the distinction between wanting to on the one hand and really wanting to, or even having to, on the other. By doing so, Mr. Shoaff did me a great favor. And after we'd talked about this, I felt for the first time I was really pointed in the direction of success. The way it happened was really simple and straightforward. Mr. Shoaff simply took me aside one day and said, "Jim, you have enough talent and intelligence to really accomplish a lot in life, but you just don't have enough reason to make it happen."

When I heard that, something clicked inside my head. This was truly a key insight, a turning point in my life. I had always doubted if I had enough ability to be successful. But suddenly I realized that having enough ability was not the problem—the problem was having enough reason.

I'm no Victor Herman. Frankly, I doubt whether you are either. We don't have the willpower to achieve success in a vacuum, as if we were standing out in the middle of a Siberian forest loading logs. We need all the help we can get in terms of motivation.

FOUR POWERFUL MOTIVATORS

But, of course, different people are motivated by different things. I've read a number of studies on motivation, and the ones I found most convincing have isolated four main factors as the most powerful human motivators. I'll go through them one by one and I urge you to read each carefully. Think about how you can put them to use to help you to accomplish your goals.

If you are in a managerial or leadership position, think also about how you can use them to help the people you are supervising. These are the real factors that make people get off their behinds and do things. These are what work when *wanting to* just isn't enough. These are the true reasons for believing something is worth doing and then for actually doing it.

The first great motivator is recognition from peers. When soldiers in wartime give up their lives during combat, why do they do it? Is it because of patriotism or belief in the cause they're fighting for or fear of being court martialed if they do otherwise? Perhaps all those things play a part, but extensive research has shown that what really motivates a soldier to fight well in combat is the desire for the respect of the man fighting right beside him. This is much more important than medals or other forms of public recognition—which in the confusion of wartime, are often given to the wrong people anyway.

What motivates soldiers in combat is only an extreme version of what motivates sales associates on the floor of a car dealership, students in a classroom, or a team of lawyers trying to win a case. I don't know if this is still done, but for many years the players in the National Football League used to select their own all-star team at the end of each season. I was always interested, and rather amused, by the differences between the player selection and the all-star team picked by the fans or sportswriters. I'm certain that the honor of being selected by one's fellow players meant a lot more than any sort of recognition from someone sitting up in the grandstands with a hotdog in his mouth. Quite simply, recognition from peers is a truly powerful motivating force in any human activity.

The second important motivator is recognition from respected experts or authorities. I can tell you that in my own life this has been an extremely important factor. Mr. Shoaff was someone I respected from the first moment I was introduced to him. He was also someone whose respect I desperately wanted to earn.

Has there been someone like that in your life? Or is there such a person in your life right now? It's important to realize that a respected expert doesn't have to be a person who is known far and wide around the world. You are the one who establishes the qualifications. Though very often, people who you find impressive will be equally impressive to others.

Once you have met such a person, or even if you have seen them from a distance, or perhaps read an article about them in the paper, don't hesitate to politely approach them and introduce yourself. Unless you happen to catch them at a particularly difficult moment, most successful people are eager to help others and to pass on what they've learned. Sure, I was apprehensive about meeting Mr. Shoaff when I first saw him, but I shudder to think what my life would be like if I hadn't approached him.

From a motivational point of view, the great thing about establishing a relationship with a mentor is that you eventually become so close that you can almost hear that person advising you, even when they are not really there. Earl Shoaff passed on years ago. He died suddenly at the age of only forty-nine, but I still feel like he's talking to me every day, and I still want to earn his approval and respect. I think it will always be that way.

Family is the third great motivator, and in many ways it's really the most powerful. Although the approval of peers and experts may be most important in your career, in your life as a whole nothing can compare with the importance of your family.

An experience I had a number of years ago is a good illustration of that principle. I had just finished giving a talk before a group of entrepreneurs in Minneapolis when a young man approached me and asked me for some advice about achieving financial success.

As I always do when asked for that sort of advice, I began with a couple of standard, straightforward questions. The first one was, how much money would you like to make annually? When I ask this question, I want to see whether the person has given enough thought to his or her goals to come up with a specific figure. That's a much better sign than someone who just says, "I want to make a whole lot." But this fellow was even more specific and focused than I could possibly have expected.

"I need to make at least a quarter of a million dollars a year for the next ten years," he said without a second's hesitation.

"And why do you want to make that amount?" I now inquired. This was another standard question of mine.

And once again he answered immediately, "Mr. Rohn," he said, "ten years from now when my kids are old enough to enjoy it, I want to take my family on a trip around the world that they will remember all of their lives. The trip itself will last for twelve full months with no expenses spared. And in order to save enough money to make it happen, I will need an annual income of two hundred and fifty thousand dollars for the next decade." There were literally tears in his eyes as he said this.

Although I haven't heard from him since then, I have no doubt he achieved his goal. In my mind's eye, I could picture him over the coming years working long hours, meeting deadlines, overcoming obstacles, doing everything it takes to be successful today, and doing it gladly. After all, he was motivated by something more than just a simple desire for financial success and the material rewards that come with it. This man was working because he desired to give his wife and children a lifetime's worth of priceless memories. And if that isn't a reason to believe, I don't know what is. Someone who can feel that level of emotions for other human beings is truly blessed. And the family who has that sort of spouse and parent is truly blessed as well.

The fourth and last achievement motivating factor is the impulse toward benevolence—a desire to benefit the family of humankind. It is closely related to the desire to benefit your family, of sharing your wealth and wisdom with the world.

I'm fond of Andrew Carnegie's life story, the Scottish immigrant who founded the United States Steel Company in the 1800s. When Carnegie died, a yellow sheet of paper was found in his desk on which he had written a note to himself when he was still in his twenties. This note set forth the main goal of his life. It read, "I'm going to spend the first half of my life accumulating money. And I'm going to spend the last half of my life giving it all away." Did this impulse toward benevolence provide to be a strong motivator for success? At age sixty-five, he sold the steel company for $480 million (worth about $13 billion today) and devoted the rest of his life to philanthropic activities. During his lifetime, Carnegie gave away over $350 million (worth about $4.8 billion today), including more than $56 million to build 2,500 libraries worldwide.

When we look at the four important motivators, what do we really see? I immediately noticed that they all involve other people, whether peers, mentors, family members, or simply fellow members of the human race. It's ironic, isn't it? To be successful, you need the very internal, very personal, very unique quality called strong character. But to acquire that innermost quality and set it to work, you need people other than yourself as reasons to believe.

Maybe that's not true if you're the toughest man on earth. Maybe then you could do whatever needs to be done just because you set your mind to do it. Yet, there is only one toughest man on earth at any one time, and I'm not the one. I'm kind of glad about that, too, because needing and working for other people is really what made my life worthwhile. And I'm sure you feel the same way.

ETHICAL LIVING

Within each person there is a kind of imaginary measuring instrument. I'm not sure if it's a scale, calculator, compass, or a combination of all three, but it's always working, always taking readings, always balancing temptations of every kind—and there are many, many kinds—against the benefits of living ethically and with strong character. When the temptations outweigh the benefits, that's all it takes for some very unfortunate things to start happening.

In my opinion, and I think there are very few exceptions to this, a bad person is somebody who simply doesn't have enough reasons to be good. Throughout this book you've read about all the ways in which other people and your attachments to them can help build character and success. Now I'd like to show you how each one represents a definite commitment on your part, a risk, an investment that you know you will lose if you fail to live up to the standard you have set for yourself.

Every time you make that commitment, every time you take that risk, you tip the balance of that internal scale back in the direction of character, steadfastness, and doing the right thing. After all, whenever you make a commitment to one of the traits we've discussed here, in a sense, you are making an investment. So if you were to start living in ways that run counter to those traits, you will lose the investment, wouldn't you? No one likes to lose investments. Once that starts happening, it's not long before you're broke.

AN UNSHAKABLE AND INDESTRUCTIBLE LIFESTYLE

The unshakable and indestructible foundation upon which to build your successful and fulfilling life and career includes: courage, honesty, integrity, perseverance, wisdom, responsibility, humor, flexibility, patience, confidence, good health, achievement—all adding up to a strong character. Let's briefly look at each one again as a refresher—and to really commit each to your everyday way of living.

Courage was the first quality of strong character we discussed. Courage is not the absence of fear. It is indeed the presence of fear for the right reasons at the right time and of the right thing. We should not fear failure, for example. Anyone can fail and virtually everyone does at one time or another. Many outstanding leaders in every walk of life have failed many times and have gone on to greatness nonetheless. If we fear anything, it should only be to fear failure to do our best. We should fear failure to live up to the ideals we've set for ourselves. A great poet wrote, "All men would be cowards if they were brave enough." I think there is some truth to that. So embrace your fear—take it inside yourself and use it as a foundation for true courage.

We then considered a pair of qualities that are closely related—*honesty and integrity*. We saw how telling the truth can be painful in the same way that paying off a debt can be painful. There's a temptation to hedge and equivocate, just as there is a temptation to run up large balances on credit cards. But credit buying doesn't make long-term sense in either finances or ethics. In both areas, the interest charges will eat you up. But in the first case, it's only your bank balance that will be destroyed. In the second case, it's your soul.

Perseverance was our next element of strong character. We saw how reserve energy is the mark of strong character in any field of endeavor, and how successful people manage to reach down into themselves for the strength to overcome any challenge, whether external or internal. Also discussed was why goals are as important to achievement as a net, a baseline, or keeping score is to tennis. You may become an excellent player without them, but that's not likely. And anyway, how would you ever know?

We considered *responsibility* as an element of strong character and saw how most people will do almost anything to avoid it. Yet individuals who seek out responsibility, those who want the ball when the game is on the line, can gain material and spiritual rewards that naturally flow from strong character and the glory that comes with leadership.

In our discussion of *wisdom*, we saw why the desire for it can never be satisfied—and why that very impossibility makes wisdom even more desirable to those who truly love it. Socrates and Solomon, though different in many ways, were united in their ability to act wisely. And you read about Socrates' seemingly foolish decision to die unnecessarily was really the fullest expression of his doctrine that "Wisdom is knowing thy self."

Humor, though not often considered a quality of strong character, has proven to be a very important one. Particularly in this country, the ability to laugh at one's self is evidence of trustworthiness and fundamental integrity. We also saw why humor must be handled carefully, and that there is quite a difference between saying something funny and being funny.

We looked at *flexibility* as an element of character and why it's critical for success in every human undertaking. Flexibility is strength without rigidity. It means recognizing what can be controlled and what is beyond our control, and behaving accordingly. It means playing the cards that we are dealt as best we can and resisting the temptation to think that the deck is stacked against us.

Patience, like flexibility, was discussed as an aspect of character that helps us to not only cope with the unpredictability of fate, but allows us to turn them into the materials of success. Patience is the quality that allows us to enlist time as an ally instead of fighting hopelessly against it as an adversary. Patience is the hallmark of true maturity and distinguishes strong character from the weak, and the mature adult from the unfinished and unformed child—whether the person is three or thirty-three.

Confidence is both an intrinsic element of character and an emotional commodity to be invested in others. Confidence is the ability to inspire trust. Yet it can only be achieved by trusting both in yourself and in the people you meet. If you are truly a confident person, your belief in yourself is strong enough so that the world itself seems safe and oriented toward your success. Confidence is one aspect of a strong character that can literally change the way we perceive reality.

Good health is an aspect of strong character because it springs from wise choices. It's neither a religion, a diet, an exercise program, or the number of calories we have consumed in a twenty-four-hour period. Rather, good health expresses an awareness of who we are and how we should live in the most fundamental sense.

And we examined how achievement identifies a strong character in the same way that blossoming fruit identifies a healthy tree. By taking to heart the principles and techniques that you've read, you most certainly can build an unshakable character—and I have no doubt that success of every kind will follow. Because I have no doubt of that, I close this book with a few thoughts about how to handle success graciously and wisely when it comes.

HANDLE SUCCESS GRACIOUSLY AND WISELY

As you struggle to achieve your goals, work to break out of old behavior patterns, and overcome inevitable obstacles, I'm in favor of using any means necessary to make progress as long as it is legal and ethical. If you want to motivate yourself with anger, and many people do this, I say go with whatever works. If you feel you've been wronged at various points in your career and you look forward to gaining sweet revenge once you reach the top, I say whatever gets you going.

But I also say, when you do achieve success, put all that behind you. Take the anger you used as fuel to climb to the top of the pinnacle, and throw it back down to the bottom. That's an act of strong character, really strong character. But it's also just plain smart. Do whatever it takes to get where you want to go—and when you get there, live well. That's your concern, to live well with courage, honesty, integrity, perseverance, responsibility, wisdom, humor, flexibility, patience, confidence, good health, and achievement.

Your concern is to build an unshakable character on a solid foundation. Once you've built it, keep it strong. And I have no doubt that you will do exactly that.

Conclusion

PERSONAL INTERVIEW WITH JIM ROHN

Jim Rohn has been described as "America's Foremost Business Philosopher." For more than thirty years, Jim shared his message with more than five thousand audiences and three million people. He established an unparalleled reputation as a dynamic and memorable speaker, focusing on the areas of personal development, success, and achieving full potential in life.

Peter Low is known as an entrepreneurial genius, having taken a company from zero sales to over $10 million in annual sales. From U.S. Presidents to Fortune 500 CEOs, from Super Bowl-winning coaches to Pulitzer Prize-winning authors, Peter has interviewed and studied the success strategies of the top achievers of the world. The following is an interesting and inspirational interview with two people with unshakable characters.

Peter Low: Jim, you are a phenomenal person in the field of teaching people how to achieve success. You've been doing it for many decades and have a very unique story. Please share that with us.

Jim Rohn: I grew up in Idaho, farm country, little small village, southwest corner of Idaho. My father still lives on the old homestead where I grew up, overlooking the Snake River. He'll be ninety-two his next birthday and he still hasn't retired. I went to high school, graduated, went to college one year; then foolishly, halfway through my second year, I decided I was smart enough and quit. Got a job, went to work. A little while later I got married, started a family, and worked hard doing what I thought was the best I could...

But year by year I kept falling a little farther behind. Purchasing more than I could pay for on time, the creditors starting to call once in a while saying, "Hey, you told us the check was in the mail." I'm getting embarrassed by it all but didn't really know what to do.

By the time I reached age twenty-five, I had only pennies in my pocket, nothing in the bank, behind on my big-mouth promises to my family, not feeling good about myself, and wondering what could I do to make my life better. I thought about going back to school, but with a family it was a tough decision. I thought, *Gosh if I had a business of my own, that would do it.* But I had no money. Then good fortune came my way. It's difficult sometimes to explain good fortune, why something remarkable happens at a particular time.

But my good fortune was, at age twenty-five, I met a very wealthy man. His name was Mr. Earl Shoaff. A friend of mine worked for him and told me about Mr. Shoaff. He said, "You gotta meet this man. He's rich but he's easy to talk to. And he's got a remarkable philosophy of life." And my friend kept going on and on about Mr. Shoaff.

I had a chance a little later to meet Mr. Shoaff, and I was impressed. He was rich, obviously, but he was easy to talk to.

Within a few minutes, I'm dazzled. And I thought, *I'd give anything if I could be like that. Rich and easy to talk to. What would that take? If I could just get around somebody like him, then if he would teach me and coach me, I would learn it all.* And that was my good fortune.

A little while later this rich man hired me, and I spent five years in his employ. Unfortunately, he died at the end of that five years, age forty-nine. But I spent five years with this wealthy man—the last five of his life and the first five years of my new life. My dream came true. He coached me, taught me which books to read, the disciplines and the skills I needed. He taught me about the major changes I needed to make in my language and personality. What he shared with me during those five years revolutionized my life, changed my income, changed my bank account, changed my future. I've never been the same.

By the time I was thirty-one I was a millionaire. That was just my money. What was really valuable were the skills and the disciplines I had acquired. When I was living in Beverly Hills, a friend of mine said one day, "Jim, you have to come and tell your story to my service club, the Rotary Club. A boy from the farms of Idaho now living in Beverly Hills. What a story. If I arranged it, would you come and talk at our breakfast meeting?"

And I said, "Sure." I went and made a presentation and they liked it. By the time the day was finished, my phone rang two more times. Other clubs called, asking, "Would you tell us that story?" So before long, I was spending a piece of my business time giving breakfast and luncheon talks.

Then one day, a man who had heard my talk about three times said, "Would you come and talk to my management and salespeople? If you would, I'd be happy to pay you."

207

And I thought, *Wow, wouldn't that be something? Tell my story and get paid.*

He arranged it, I went and shared my story, got paid, and little did I know another fortune was waiting for me to share my story. It turned into a business. I'm primarily an entrepreneur, and this is now one of my most flourishing businesses.

Peter Low: One of the things I always look for in people who are successful, is not people who are successful for one year or two years, but people who have long-lasting success. There are so many people who learned to be successful and then they lose it. How have you been able to endure all these thirty-three years so successfully?

Jim Rohn: Well, I get the question, "Doesn't it get old after a while?" But it really doesn't. I have plenty of other business projects to work on. I really don't need to lecture. But the ideas that I share with people these days so dramatically affected my own life back in those early days that I never get tired of sharing the story and the principles.

I enjoy sharing what changed my income, my bank account, my outlook on life, got me setting goals, building a library, working on disciplines that I never thought I could master—in sharing all those ideas with people, then getting the appreciative letters and phone calls...ahh, it's all worth it. When I travel around the world people still come up and say, "You know five years ago I attended your seminar, and here's what happened...." A lady showed me the other day a note she wrote in Australia that she had written fourteen years ago. She said, "I still use these notes in working in my business. Here's what happened to my relationship with my family." Those letters, those phone calls, those personal testimonials, for me, that's what I live for. I don't need the money. I take the money, but I don't need the money.

But I do need the joy that comes from people saying, "What you said was valuable for me, and thank you very much for sharing." That's heavy-weight stuff, you can't buy it with money.

Peter Low: I once interviewed Senator Teddy Kennedy and asked him, "What is the secret to your success?" And without batting an eye he said, "Perseverance." And I'm sure you know the quote of Benjamin Disraeli where he said, "The secret to success is constancy of purpose." You are somebody who has really exemplified perseverance and constancy of purpose. What would you say to somebody who says, "I don't feel like I can persevere? I don't really seem to have a deep-down purpose that I can hone in on and stay with for decades to come."

Jim Rohn: Well, it has to be from a variety of sources. You have to have family goals, you have to have personal goals, worthy projects you would like to support. It's not just income goals. It's not to have a home, a nice car, and clothes to wear. It's the full variety of things. You can develop an appetite for all of that. I call them reasons. Reasons make the difference. If you have enough reasons, you can do spectacular things.

There is an ancient script that says, "Without a vision, we die." If I can get people caught up in thinking about where they would like to go, who they would like to meet, the kind of income they would like to have, the kind of money they would like to share, the kind of skills they would like to develop, the influence they would like to have, the reputation they like to build—Would you like to be an entrepreneur? Would you like to have a masterful management career? Would you like to be a better parent? What kind of influence would you like to

209

have on the people around you? Would you like to influence the industry you are in?—they find that there's a whole wide range of things to accomplish.

That is called the promise of the future. Without that promise, life becomes a little less worth living. If the promise is clear, we will pay the disciplines, we will pay the price, we will read the books, we will take the classes, we'll learn the skills. That is one of the first things—articulate the promise. A big job parents have these days is getting kids to see the promise of the future, the possibilities, the opportunities.

Peter Low: What is the promise of the future for your life, Jim?

Jim Rohn: To write a lot more books, see a lot more places, talk to a lot more people, enjoy my family. I have two grand-kids. Nathaniel is eight and Natalie is six-and-a-half. And I have two daughters; I have some very special friends I want to spend a lot of time with. My father is my business partner at age ninety-one.

But in my entrepreneurial career, I have a lot of things I want to accomplish; some products I want to develop, some places I want to visit. But in my speaking career, I just want to reach everyone I can. Now I'm getting interested in kids. I'd like to develop a lot more products for teenagers; home study courses on personal development, financial planning, setting goals, those are some of my goals for the future. They keep me going.

Peter Low: One of your products I think is so phenomenal is your book, *A Treasury of Quotes*. It comes with beautiful gold foil printing on the cover. What would you say are some of the quotes that have really impacted your life?

Jim Rohn: When I used to cross my fingers and say, "I sure hope things will change for me," my mentor, Mr. Shoaff would say, "Mr. Rohn, for things to change for you, *you* have to change." I used to hope the economy would change, or my boss would change and become more benevolent. I used to hope that circumstances would change, that difficulties would go away. But he would say, "Things aren't going to change. It's going to be like it has always been. But if *you* will change; everything will change for you. If you'll get better, everything will get better for you."

That is more or less the centerpiece of the philosophy I've been trying to teach all these years. And I think that is one of the best quotes. It is a promise he gave me—If you will change, everything will change for you.

But if you won't change, the next five years will probably be just about like the last five. But anytime you want to, you can learn from the last five and make the next five years of your life totally different from the last five. If you will make some little simple beginning changes—for your health, for your income, being more valuable in the marketplace, things you want for yourself and your family, and all of the rest, life will be different.

Peter Low: Let's say I have a bad habit, and I want to change. How do I do that?

Jim Rohn: Small pieces at a time. The best is to substitute a poor habit with a good habit. If you have a bad habit as far as your health is concerned, start some good ones. My mama taught, "An apple a day keeps the doctor away." And my father will be ninety-two, he's never been ill. I've never been ill, my children, my grandchildren, Mama taught us so well. Those simple, basic good habits of good health that we've followed all of these years. And the payoff is extraordinary. So maybe you have something like smoking that you shouldn't do. Rather than just trying to quit, start something positive and you will get so inspired about doing the new thing that you will change your negative habit into a positive habit.

Peter Low: How would you define success? What does it really mean to be successful?

Jim Rohn: For me, success is simply the steady progress toward predetermined goals. Success is not a stereotype—you have to live in a certain home, drive a certain car, earn certain money, have money in the bank, that's really not success. If a man says to me, "Hey, I'm soon going to cash it all in, I'm headed for the mountains. I'm going to live off of the land. I'm going to feed the squirrels the rest of my life." And if he cashes it in and goes and does that, to me he is a smashing success. We might not call him *successful* if we looked at his life or his lifestyle, but if he is enjoying the product of his own dreams or making progress in that direction, to me he is successful.

Success is looking at your own desires, looking at your own possibilities, and then stretching yourself to see if you can become all that you can become, earn all that you can earn, share all that you can share, make steady progress in that direction—to me, that is success.

Peter Low: You've traveled all around the world. As Americans, what are some lessons we could learn from people in other cultures concerning life and achieving true success in life?

Jim Rohn: A lot of the immigrants who come to America from other countries have taught us some great lessons. They're some of the best students in school. The Russians who came to Israel tell me now that they are the leaders in industry, they are so grateful for liberty, freedom, and a chance. They need no guarantees, they don't need to be taken care of, all they need is an open door, a ladder to climb, a place to start, somebody to give them a chance and away they go.

I think we've had it so easy in America for so long that we have lost that sharp edge. Who knows, with all the shakeup these last few years, the walls have come tumbling down. But in America, we need a whole new sense of personal drive, of personal ambition that will take whatever we have and see what we can make out of it.

If it's pennies we start with pennies, if it is painful, start painful, if you're ill, start ill, if you don't have much of a chance, you just start with not much of a chance but see what you can make of it. I think some of the people in other countries now, where freedom is finely intact, and the walls have come down, could teach us a lot about taking what we have and making something valuable out of it. Rather than expecting someone to give us something.

Peter Low: Zig Ziglar cites a study showing that legal immigrants to America are four times more likely to become millionaires than native-born Americans. I shared with you earlier how I grew up in India. I'm really grateful for that opportunity because it really underscores to me the tremendous opportunities we have in America. For the person who has always lived in America and maybe has never seen anything different, what can you say to them to really help them appreciate and be grateful for the tremendous opportunities they have?

Jim Rohn: We need to be reminded, that no country in the last six thousand years of written history has been such a depository of the gifts from the rest of the world like the

United States of America. For two hundred years the ethnic streams that have flowed into America have brought their gifts with them: the gift of liberty, the gift of freedom, the gift of politics, the gift of religion, the gift of the work ethic, the gift of music, the gift of healing, the gift of medicine, the gift of inventions, the arts, dance.

And not to appreciate those gifts or develop a cynical attitude because it came from such a diversity of ethnic streams, would be such a great mistake. If there are books provided that you don't read, classes you don't take, music you don't listen to, ideas you ignore, places of learning where you find the contact that could change your life and never take advantage of all those opportunities—that's the big tragedy. To have so much brought to your fingertips and not to be excited about it—how sad.

But that is what seminars are for, that's books are for, that's what messages like this are for, to remind people of what all is available. Let us not be cynical, let us be thankful and reach out and appropriate what's available. Let it affect our lives now and in the future.

Peter Low: I was on an airplane and I sat beside a businessman who said he had been really impacted by you—that you had said something about the story of Job that had made an impact in his life. What exactly do you tell people about Job?

Jim Rohn: Well, first I tell them that I find the Bible very fascinating. I am an amateur when it comes to the Bible. But I am fascinated by the story (not verbatim from the Bible, just my interpretation of what happened). God and Satan were visiting one day and made this deal about taking down the wall of safety from around Job. Satan said, "If you do that, I promise you very shortly your great friend Job will curse you." God said, "No way." So the wager is on and God takes the wall down according to the terms of the wager. When he does, Satan does one of his all-time famous numbers. First, he took Job's family, blow one. Second, he took Job's wealth, blow two. Third, he took Job's health, blow three.

And as if that isn't bad enough, Job's wife comes along when he is sitting in the ashes scraping his sores with a rock, and says, "Job, looks like your friend God is long gone. You might as well curse him and die." Satan said to God, "Here's when Job will curse you." While they both listen, Job says to his wife, "Never. No matter what happens, I will never curse my friend God." And God said, "I knew it!" Then God made it up to Job. According to the story, God multiplied two times what Job had before; twice the family, twice the wealth, twice the health. And Job became a very famous man in the known world in those days.

I find that interesting and fascinating. I used to find things frustrating, but I've learned a little key is to try to turn frustration into fascination. If you try hard, you can do it too. I'm on the freeway in Los Angeles, heading for the airport, my plane leaves in forty-five minutes and the traffic is moving not one inch. I am now fascinated. Now it doesn't work every time, but every time you *can* get it to work, it's fascinating. After all, it's better to be fascinated than to be frustrated.

Peter Low: And let's say that you miss the plane, are you still fascinated?

Jim Rohn: I'm fascinated by my own frustration.

Peter Low: Very good. Now what would be one of the greatest lessons you have ever learned in your life?

Jim Rohn: That true values really count. My greatest lesson is that humans are a special, unique creation. We're not like any other lifeform. We can go north, we can go south, we can go east, we can go west. We can live one way for five years and tear up that script and live another way the next five years. We are not driven by instinct and a genetic code. My study in the possibilities overwhelms me. As to where people can begin and then finally where they can go—what they can start with and what they can finally become.

And we can recognize that life is an incredibly exciting adventure. If we start working with it, we can wonder, *What could I really do if I learned the lessons, adopted the disciplines, read the books, fed on the ideas like bread for my mind? What could I really accomplish?* The stories are always fascinating about where people started but where they finally ended up, what they finally accomplished. With dangers along the way, of course. But that is what philosophy is all about. Human philosophy is to give us guidance to avoid the dangers and take advantage of the opportunities.

That is what seminars are for. That's why I teach as I do, to help people with a refined guidance system. Number one, to earlier recognize the dangers and to also, earlier, pick up the opportunities and make something of them. I am constantly amazed at the human spirit, human possibilities. People with the most enormous, struggling problems still manage to rise above them and do something noble, something powerful, something wonderous. I'm always intrigued by that.

I am intrigued with myself. How I act like I act, how I respond like I respond. What is this human adventure on the spinning planet? I'm intrigued by America—nationally, industries, commerce, business, companies, corporations, institutions, education, politics, all of the rest. I think we need to be curious about it. How it works and how we can best play our part in family, in community, as citizens, employees, business owners—all of it.

Peter Low: And how do we develop that curiosity? I remember once riding in a car with Larry King, he asked me maybe a hundred questions in a twenty-minute ride. Partly, I think, what makes him a good interviewer is he is very curious, he wants to know everything. For the rest of us, how do we develop that kind of curiosity that you talk about?

Jim Rohn: Kids have curiosity, right? That's why they learn so much that first six, seven years. Kids are studying ants, adults are walking on them, right? Kids don't walk on ants, they're studying them. How can an ant can carry something bigger than he is? That kind of curiosity; when I teach communication I start with that.

To be a good communicator, first of all, you have to have something good to say. To have something good to say, number one, we need to sharpen our interests. You have to read the paper and magazines. You have to know what is going on. Develop an appetite for current events, political events, social events. Part of that is training, and the more you do it, the more you get into it. If you establish that habit pattern, your interests will start to grow and grow and grow.

Next is fascination. Interested people want to know if it works. Fascinated people want to know how it works. Curiosity, develop an appetite for that. Just start by saying, "I'm going to systematically make some inquiry. I'm going to be a better reader. I'm going to listen better. I'm going to search." Start the whole process. The more you do it, you'll find something fascinating, that will lead to something else fascinating—and quickly you are on an upward trend.

Peter Low: You mentioned values. A *Newsweek* magazine poll shows that 76 percent of Americans think that America is on the wrong road morally and spiritually right now. I think it was Einstein who said, "Don't aim to become a person of success, aim to become a person of value." What role do values play in your life? And what role do they play in the success or failure of our lives?

Jim Rohn: Very important topic, values. In talking to teenagers, first of all I start with money to teach personal development. One, kids are interested in money. Two, it's easy to count. And here's what I say to my teenage friends, "We get paid for bringing value to the marketplace." A simple statement of economics. It takes time, but we don't get paid for the time, we get paid for the value. Now since that's true, is it possible to become twice as valuable and make twice as much money in the same time? And the answer is, yes of course. Could you become three times more valuable than you are right now and make three times as much money in the same time? And the answer is, yes of course. Could you become ten times more valuable than you are right now, to the marketplace, and make ten times as much money in the same time? Now first we're talking money, talking economics. And the answer is, yes of course.

America's economic ladder starts at, say, $5 an hour and goes up to the biggest income last year was $200 million, the guy who runs Disney. Why would the marketplace pay someone only $5 an hour? Because they are not very valuable to the marketplace. We have to emphasize *to the marketplace*. The person receiving $5 an hour might be a valuable brother, member of the family, member of the church, citizen of the country, no doubt, and valuable in the sight of God, of course, we are all of equal value in the sight of God.

But to the marketplace, if you are not very valuable, you don't get much money. Then why would the marketplace pay someone $50 an hour? *Evidently,* they must be more valuable to the marketplace. Why would the marketplace pay someone $500 an hour? And the word is, *evidently* they must be more valuable. Why would a company pay one person $200 million for a year's work? And the big word is, *evidently* this person must be very valuable. If this person helps the company make $4 billion a year, would he receive $200 million? And the answer is, of course.

Mr. Shoaff taught me how to climb this ladder and here is what he said, "Work harder on yourself than you do on your job." When I refined that bit of economic philosophy, it changed my life. Up until age twenty-five, I worked hard on my job and made a living. Starting at age twenty-five, I worked hard on myself and I made a fortune. And then I put it in a philosophical phrase, "Success is not something you pursue. Success is something you attract by the person you become. What you pursue usually alludes you, like the butterfly you can't quite catch. But if you want to be successful, you must attract success by developing the skills, the temperament. What you now know about the marketplace, goods and services, that's what's valuable. So, the key to getting paid well in the marketplace is to become valuable."

Now we must not only be valuable to the marketplace, we must create value for our family. A father must illustrate for his children the promise of the future. He must share stories and illustrations when articulating the vision, the promise, the possibilities, and the opportunities his children have. A mother showers her children with caring, heart, soul, and compassion. Value to the marketplace in terms of economics, but also value to home and family.

And then value as a citizen. Let's talk capitalism, democracy, freedom. Fortunately, we won the Cold War. But we have some other challenges now. To become valuable in articulating the challenge of the future of competing among the nations of the world, we've got our work cut out for us. It starts at home, being valuable as a teacher. Whether it's a company, corporation, government, school, community, home, family, office, basketball team, baseball team, wherever people gather, for whatever reason, if each one brings a better value to that enterprise, game, family, business, office, we have a good chance of competing well among the nations of the world. And who knows what all we can accomplish in the 21st century?

Peter Low: What is the most important change that the average person can make in life?

Jim Rohn: Start with something simple. Mama said, "An apple a day keeps the doctor away." What if what she said is true? Someone says, "Well if that's true, that would be easy to do." But here is the challenge, what's easy to do is easy *not* to do. What if you should be walking around the block every day for your good health and you don't. If you should and you could, and you don't, it's called a formula for disaster. Self-improvement is starting with the most immediate thing that comes to your mind that you could do to improve your health, your life, your income, your future. And if it's an apple a day, start there. If it's a walk around the block, start there.

If you need to build your personal development library, go get a book and say, "This is the next book of my new library." If you need to attend a seminar, go. If you need to keep a journal, start writing. Mr. Shoaff taught me to keep a journal, starting at age twenty-five. My own journals represent a major part of my library; also notes that I've copied over the years, little poems I've written down, things I've gathered that are invaluable to me, my business, as well as my lecturing career.

Go get a journal. Start with an apple a day. A walk around the block. Positive change is not going to come in some great package out of the sky. Each little thing you start with called self-improvement matters. Whether it's health or signing up for a class that you've been intending to take and you've put off. Neglect does us all in. Neglect has us by the throat, shutting off air supply, money supply, and every other supply. But if you reverse that process, you will see a positive difference in your life. Instead of saying, "I should, I could, I don't." Now you will say, "I could, I would, I will!"

If it's an apple a day, start there. Get a journal, make an entry. Buy a book and put it in your thriving library. Sign up for a class. You have now begun the process. And that's all you need to do—begin the process. The early return from those early steps will inspire you to start taking all the rest.

Peter Low: Now what about the people who are movers and shakers, those who have already achieved incredible success, they seem to be doing almost everything right or certainly far better than the average person. What do you say to them?

Jim Rohn: Everything needs refinement. I have a good phrase, "Everything by longevity tends to get off course." When they make a shot for the moon, the early guidance system doesn't last all the way. They have what they call, mid-course corrections. There isn't anything that doesn't need to be looked at, fairly often.

I've heard more than one person say, "Hey, I have plenty of money in the bank, I'm doing well." But some systems are not working and failure to take a look at some systems that aren't working, you can get faked out by money in the bank. You have to look at all areas.

An ancient script says, "The little foxes spoil the vines." You may look at your vineyard and it looks great—but all systems need to be regularly checked. Big gambling houses in Las Vegas draw up a financial profit and loss statements several times a day! So much is happening that they can't let more than a few hours go by before they take another look, take another look. Our lives and our businesses are far more valuable than a gambling house in Las Vegas. But what a good lesson. So don't let too much time go by before you take a look to make sure that all systems are working, including your health, relationships, business and household accounts, whatever, you will be better off for the future.

Peter Low: That's tremendous advice, Jim. Now in closing, is there anything else you would like to share with our Success Talk listeners?

Jim Rohn: It's my privilege to share my story. I take great delight in sharing what happened to me in some simple way that might be valuable to someone else. But my last word would be: start with something simple, keep adding value to your life, and you can do the most extraordinary things. And why not you? If a boy from the farms of Idaho can, why not you? We started with nothing, why not you? We started from behind, why not you? If we can do it, you can do it. That's my message.

ABOUT THE AUTHOR

JIM ROHN (1930-2009)

For more than 40 years, Jim Rohn honed his craft like a skilled artist—helping people the world over sculpt life strategies that expanded their imagination of what is possible. Those who had the privilege of hearing him speak can attest to the elegance and common sense of his material.

It is no coincidence, then, that he is still widely regarded as one of the most influential thinkers of our time, and thought of by many as a national treasure. He authored countless books and audio and video programs and helped motivate and shape an entire generation of personal-development trainers and hundreds of executives from America's top corporations.

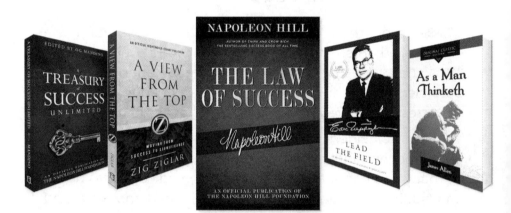